CULTURE SMART!
PANAMA

Heloise Crowther

·K·U·P·E·R·A·R·D·

First published in Great Britain 2006
by Kuperard, an imprint of Bravo Ltd
59 Hutton Grove, London N12 8DS
Tel: +44 (0) 20 8446 2440 Fax: +44 (0) 20 8446 2441
www.culturesmartguides.com
Inquiries: sales@kuperard.co.uk

Culture Smart! is a registered trademark of Bravo Ltd

Distributed in the United States and Canada
by Random House Distribution Services
1745 Broadway, New York, NY 10019
Tel: +1 (212) 572-2844 Fax: +1 (212) 572-4961
Inquiries: csorders@randomhouse.com

Series Editor Geoffrey Chesler

ISBN 978 1 85733 339 8

British Library Cataloguing in Publication Data
A CIP catalogue entry for this book is available from the
British Library

Printed in Malaysia

This book is available for special discounts for bulk purchases for
sales promotions or premiums. Special editions, including
personalized covers, excerpts of existing books, and corporate
imprints, can be created in large quantities for special needs.

For more information in the U.S.A. write to Special
Markets/Premium Sales, 1745 Broadway, MD 6–2, New York,
NY 10019 or e-mail specialmarkets@randomhouse.com.

In the United Kingdom contact Kuperard publishers at the
above address.

Cover image: Traditional painted wooden houses on Colón Island, Panama.
Travel Ink/David Forman
The images on pages 13, 17, 36, 39, 54, 88, 91, 125, and 136 are reproduced
by permission of the author.

CultureSmart!Consulting and **Culture Smart!** guides have both
contributed to and featured regularly in the weekly travel program
"Fast Track" on BBC World TV.

About the Author

HELOISE CROWTHER is a British travel writer who specializes in Central America. Currently based in Costa Rica and London, she writes for guidebooks and English newspapers. She spent five years traveling in Latin America, and lived in Panama for three, during which time she wrote extensively about the country. Heloise was the major specialist contributor to *Panama: The Bradt Travel Guide*, which won the 2005 Best Guide Book Award from the British Guild of Travel Writers.

Other Books in the Series

Other titles are in preparation. For more information, contact: info@kuperard.co.uk

The publishers would like to thank **CultureSmart!**Consulting for its help in researching and developing the concept for this series.

CultureSmart!Consulting creates tailor-made seminars and consultancy programs to meet a wide range of corporate, public-sector, and individual needs. Whether delivering courses on multicultural team building in the U.S.A., preparing Chinese engineers for a posting in Europe, training call-center staff in India, or raising the awareness of police forces to the needs of diverse ethnic communities, we provide essential, practical, and powerful skills worldwide to an increasingly international workforce.

For details, visit www.culturesmartconsulting.com

contents

contents

Map of Panama

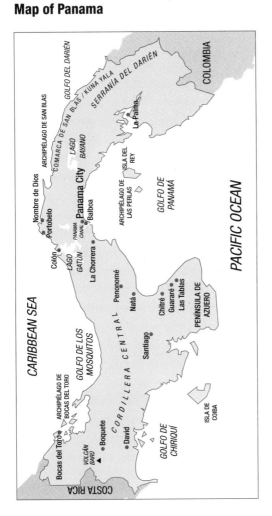

introduction

It is a long-held local belief that Panama's destiny was to serve as a gateway between East and West—and that is what this slender waist of the American world has offered ever since its discovery by Europeans in the sixteenth century. From simple paths, through rail tracks, to its great strategic waterway, the isthmus of Panama has long provided a passage between the Atlantic and Pacific Oceans, and the Panama Canal today conveys huge "Panamax" container ships carrying an immense amount of international trade.

It is likely that Spanish *conquistadores*, at the time of their first settlement on the Pacific coast, adopted the name "Panamá" from the native peoples of the region. It means "abundance of fish" —fitting for a landmass lapped by two vast oceans.

Panama's geography has not only been a vital factor in its economic well-being, but has also determined its cultural complexity. This narrow strip of land has long attracted visitors from many corners of the globe. Colonists, immigrants, and nomadic travelers have all contributed to the broad cultural and ethnic diversity that is one of the country's most outstanding and attractive attributes, and is reflected in its many customs and traditions.

Panama has, remarkably, preserved much of its indigenous Indian culture. This unique way of life continues to thrive alongside the imprint of two centuries of development. Small though it is, Panama combines the latest technology and modern commerce with an environmentally and anthropologically rich heritage. This means that you can be in the fast-moving metropolis of Panama City, and yet be less than an hour's flight away from dense rain forests and the almost unchanged life of the indigenous people.

Despite continuous foreign domination in the past, the Panamanians now have complete sovereignty over their country. Masters in their own house at last, they are both proud and welcoming. Good manners are as important to them as the original laid-back Latin style, and you will find them friendly, polite, and relaxed.

Culture Smart! Panama hopes to enrich your experience by offering insights into Panamanian society and sensibilities, and practical advice on how to behave in different situations. It describes the historical background, values and attitudes, and Panamanian life at work and at home. The better you come to know these resourceful and hospitable people, the warmer will be your welcome.

Key Facts

Official Name	República de Panamá (Republic of Panama)	
Capital City	Panama City	Population approx. 1.6 million
Other Major Cities	Colón City, David	
Area	30,193 sq. miles (78,200 sq. km)	Land: 29,339 sq. miles (75,990 sq. km) Water: 853 sq. miles (2,210 sq. km)
Geography	Lies between North and Central and South America. Shares border with Costa Rica to the NE and Colombia to the SE	Geographic coordinates: 9°00' N, 80°00' W
Terrain	Coastal plains and mountainous interior; tropical rainforest in E and NW. Pearl Islands in the Gulf of Panama; the Panama Canal	
Climate	Tropical. Dry Pacific, wet and humid Caribbean	
Population	Approx. 3,039,150 (July 2005)	
Life Expectancy	74.9 years (average male and female)	
Ethnic Makeup	*Mestizo* (mixed Amerindian and white) 70%; Amerindian and mixed (West Indian) 14%; White 10%; Indigenous 6%	

Language	Spanish	
Religion	Roman Catholic 85% Protestant 15%	
Government	Constitutional Democracy	There are 9 provinces and 3 autonomous Indian *comarcas* (territories).
Currency	Balboa. 1 balboa=100 centisimos (often called centavos, or cents)	The balboa has parity with the U.S. dollar, and U.S dollar bills and coins are used. No Panamanian paper money is issued, but coins are minted.
Media	The main television networks are Telemetro, RPC Televisión, TVN, FETV Canal 5.	The newspapers with the widest circulation are *La Prensa, El Panamá América, La Estrella de Panamá, Diario el Universal de Panamá,* and *La Crítica.*
Media: English Language	*The Panama News,* an online newspaper, www.thepanamanews.com; the *Miami Herald*	
Electricity	110 volts, 60 Hz A/C. There are repeated power surges, and use of a "surge protector" is recommended.	Panama uses North American plugs. European appliances will need adaptors.
Telephone	The country code is 507.	To dial out of Panama dial 00.
Time Zone	US Eastern Standard Time all year. (GMT-5)	

chapter one

LAND &
PEOPLE

A GEOGRAPHICAL SNAPSHOT

Panama lies between North and Central America
and South America. Like a solitary wisp of hair
growing above South America's vast continental
face, the narrow isthmus of Panama is connected
with Colombia by a mere 140-mile (225-km)
border, and covers a total area of 30,193 sq. miles
(78,200 sq. km)—roughly the same size as
Scotland. The country's political importance,
however, is disproportionate, as Panama's great
freshwater canal, which splits the country at its
narrowest point, provides a vital central crossing
point for global traffic.

The northwest of Panama has a border with
Costa Rica 205 miles (330 km) long, and the
isthmus lies almost horizontally, parallel to the
equator, between the Caribbean Sea to the north
and the north Pacific Ocean to the south, with
coastlines totaling 1,547 miles (2,490 km) in
length. Working inward from Colombia, the dense
tropical rain forest of the Darién, veined with
jungle canals and waterways, gradually thins

westward toward central Panama. Rural farmland covers much of the central interior, which rises to the central highlands: a region of mountains, forested valleys, and coffee and fruit plantations. Panama's Pacific coast is much drier than its Caribbean side, which is humid and tropical. Both coasts are strewn with islands and atolls, ranging from the rocky and cavernous to paradisiacal palm-laden mounds and slivers of golden sand.

CLIMATE

In Panama it is sometimes hard to escape unpleasant humidity, which is due to the country's proximity to the equator. Coastal areas are often cooled by sea breezes, and are always more comfortable. The temperature throughout the country fluctuates between 89 and 95°F (approx. 32 and 35°C) during the day, dropping by around 50°F (10°C) at night. In the central highlands, days are sunny but cool, and temperatures fall much further at night.

May to November is considered Panama's rainy season, when on average it rains twelve days a month. Officially, the dry season starts during December and lasts until mid-April, but in the Caribbean regions the rains may continue. This should not put visitors off; temperamental as Caribbean rainstorms may be, they tend to come and go quickly, or just happen at night. Rain is more orderly in the southern, Pacific regions, where the wet and dry seasons are more marked.

GOVERNMENT

The Republic of Panama is a constitutional democracy and a sovereign and independent state. The government consists of the executive, which includes the country's president and two vice presidents; the independent judiciary; and the legislative assembly. The president and vice presidents are elected by direct vote for a five-year term. The country is divided into nine individually governed provinces—which are further divided into sixty-seven districts—and three near- or semiautonomous Indian *comarcas* (territories).

THE PANAMANIANS

The majority of Panama's population is now comprised of *mestizos*—those who are descended from a mix of Spanish and European settlers with natives from Central America. Minority groups include blacks and native Indians. Blacks are the descendants of African slaves brought by the Spanish to Panama in the early colonial days, and of West Indian migrants who some centuries later contributed to the construction of the Panama Canal and then the booming banana trade.

Many indigenous and native peoples disappeared in the centuries following the Spanish conquest. The invasion, along with European diseases that natives had never before encountered, caused entire tribes to be wiped out—their indigenous knowledge, languages, and customs vanishing with them.

Several native Indian groups remain in Panama today: Kuna, Emberá, Wounaan, Ngöbe Buglé (also known as Guaymí), Teribe, and Bokota. While Panama now recognizes the importance of these rare cultures, anthropologists fear their future is threatened. Urban sprawl and deforestation mean that the number of Indians merging into mainstream urban life will increase. Today, native groups collectively account for around 6 percent of Panama's population.

Kuna

The Kuna (estimated population 47,000) are probably Panama's most renowned ethnic group, although they are not the largest. Originally from Colombia, they now occupy the San Blas Archipelago on the northeast Caribbean coast, and parts of the surrounding mainland, named Kuna Yala. They are subsistence farmers who survive on homegrown vegetables, grains, and fruits, and local fishing. Like all Panamanian Indians, the Kuna are skilled at wood carving and build boats and tools that are integral to their existence. Famous for their community strength, they have had to fight, throughout the centuries, to retain the rights to the land they inhabit.

The most notable event occurred in 1938 after the Kuna refused to obey government orders to integrate into Panamanian society. They proved willing to go to war to maintain their traditional lifestyle and were assisted by the U.S. military who happened to have marines stationed in the area. The Panamanian government backed down, and the Kuna people were awarded complete political and social autonomy. Their success has since inspired other indigenous Latin American groups to battle for official recognition.

Kuna people are particularly sensitive to the threat to their traditions and to their natural surroundings, and have recently imposed regulations on visitors. These are mainly obvious, such as not to leave litter or remove flora and fauna. Additionally, visitors have to ask permission to take photographs of Kuna people, and a small fee will usually be expected for this. These requirements should be respected. While other areas of Panama are being developed, the Kuna are working for the conservation of the country's threatened rain forests and have already protected nearly 150,000 acres (around 60,000 hectares) of land and organized an education center for rain forest management. It is likely that their region of Panama will be one of the few natural areas left intact in the whole country.

Kuna dress consists of a brightly colored fabric tunic and skirt. The tunics have a particularly ornate front panel, the *mola* (blouse), which is an intricately designed and hand-stitched appliqué, usually depicting natural forms such as growing seeds and wildlife. *Molas* are sold as souvenirs throughout the country. Kuna women also adorn their ankles and wrists with tiny colored beads strung together in wide bands to create patterns. Jewelry is an important part of their dress, and heavy gold nose rings are customary.

While most Kuna live in Kuna Yala, many have migrated across the country. Kuna women in traditional dress shopping on Central Avenue in Panama City, with their children dressed in modern fashions, are an everyday sight.

Emberá and Wounaan

The Emberá and Wounaan, like the Kuna, originated in Colombia, and are similar in culture to the Chocoan people (see below). They have a hunter-gatherer lifestyle, covering miles of winding jungle waterways to hunt and trade with other communities. Like the Kuna, the Emberá and Wounaan are working to protect their surrounding forests, in this case the Darién, which straddles the Colombian border. The Panamanian government has now designated more than 741,000 acres (around 300,000 hectares) of their Darién home the *Comarca* Emberá-Drua.

The Emberá and Wounaan, with an estimated population of 17,600, lead more private lives than the Kuna, chiefly because the Darién jungle is far less accessible to visitors than the San Blas islands, and thus unsuitable for vacations. However, in 1975 a small Emberá community journeyed from the Darién to the banks of the Chagres River, just outside Panama City, where they resettled. They have recently begun to open their village to tourists on a daily basis and it is now possible to observe their traditions there firsthand.

Ngöbe and Buglé

Panama's largest native group, made up of the Ngöbe and Buglé people, with an estimated population of 125,000, are often referred to as one: Ngöbe Buglé. Inhabiting the provinces of Chiriquí, Veraguas, and Bocas del Toro, they have also become known collectively as Guaymí. However, this is not a name that exists in their language, and you may offend them if you use it.

Ngöbe Buglé people retain a traditional farming and hunting lifestyle, although in some areas today many have become integrated into mainstream society, chiefly through trade. Their dress is much simpler than the dress of the Kuna and Emberá. The women wear simple, brightly colored cotton dresses that reach to the ankles, usually with some colored cotton patchwork on the shoulders and bodice and along the hem.

A BRIEF HISTORY

For such a small country, Panama's history is extensive and dramatic. Since the Spanish conquest, Panama's chronicles sound more like an epic work of fiction than historical fact. From great colonial powers to marauding pirates, Panama has suffered global interventions and foreign dominance for five centuries.

Pre-Columbian Life

The first inhabitants of the Americas were migrants from Asia. Groups traveled south through Central America and the earliest settlers are believed to have reached Panama around 12,000 BCE. Despite later Spanish looting, many pre-Columbian artifacts have survived and are testament to the creativity and intellectual output of Panama's earliest cultures.

Archaeologists believe that some of the first pottery-making villages were established in Panama, and pre-Columbian examples of pots, plates, jugs, and tribal figures and statues have been unearthed across the country. The Monagrillo culture was among the earliest discovered and is dated around the third century BCE. The most spectacular finds have been in the regions of Cocles and Chiriquí. Larger items found in Chiriquí include volcanic stone ritual tables and life-size figures from the Bariles culture (fifth century CE). Pottery remains show a range of colors from dark chocolate to rich orange and terracotta. They display tribal art using backgrounds and subjects taken from nature, such as water, sky, plants, animals, and birds.

Additionally a great amount of gold has been found in Panama, pointing to trade existing within the Americas in pre-Columbian times. Gold artifacts such as heavy tribal jewelry, breastplates, and talismans have been dug up from tombs and burial sites and are now collectively named *huacas*. Many of these items depict animals, birds, and medicine figures, or shamans, each believed to represent an important part of life. The frog shows fertility, the crocodile strength, the shaman wisdom and power. Most of the ancient gold is believed to have been looted by the Spanish, and what is left today is displayed in Panama City's anthropological museum.

During these early centuries Panama was already becoming a grand central station for migrating peoples, although historians believe the main inhabitants were those of the Chibchan, Cueva, and Chocoan peoples, communities that occupied land from Costa Rica to Colombia.

The *Conquistadores*

In 1501, Rodrigo de Bastidas became the first European to step on to Panamanian soil. However, the first major European mark on the country was made by Columbus, who arrived on Panama's northern shores in 1502. He spent the following year futilely searching for a strait between Europe and Asia that he believed to be in the country. Some areas today, from Bocas del Toro to Portobelo, still bear the names he gave them. He was ultimately frustrated in his search and never found a way across the isthmus. Despite returning to Spain unfulfilled, Columbus was the first to encounter Panamanian peoples and culture.

In 1513 Vasco Núñez de Balboa sealed Panama's future for many generations. The first European to cross the isthmus on foot, Balboa claimed the country for the Spanish crown. As in other parts of Latin America, the arrival of the Spanish *conquistadores* drastically changed the face of the country. Battles and, most importantly, diseases, against which native peoples had no resistance, wiped out numerous tribes. Loss of life in Panama escalated to the extent that colonial European settlers sent for Indian slaves from neighboring countries.

The Colonial Era and the Shipment of Treasures
The Spanish moved in quickly, founding Panamá Vieja, the first European settlement on America's Pacific coast, in 1519. When the gold of the Incas was discovered in South America, Panama opened up one of the world's major trade routes—one that would remain just as important for centuries to come. Gold and treasure were shipped to Panama's new capital city and then transported overland to the Caribbean port of Nombre de Dios, from where they were shipped on to Europe. Panama's narrow center provided a short land crossing, and the Spanish-constructed path

was named the Camino Real. However, the route was far from trouble-free, and pirates and bounty hunters continually threatened the shipments of gold. In 1668 the Welsh buccaneer Henry Morgan sacked and stole enough "pieces of eight" from Portobelo to make them legal tender in nearby Jamaica. In 1671, he crossed the isthmus and looted Panamá Vieja itself; the city was completely destroyed by fire in the attack. Panama City was rebuilt in a new, fortified position on the Pacific, known today as Casco Viejo (or San Felipe).

Vision of a Waterway
The Spanish determined to find an alternative to the Camino Real, which was regularly attacked by bandits and subject to the encroachments of dense jungle. They had plans for a waterway connecting the two oceans as early as 1524, and numerous surveys were carried out to consider the different possibilities. The Camino de Cruces was constructed as an early attempt and linked the Camino Real with the Chagres River, greatly shortening the overland distance. This was as far as the Spanish managed to get, however, and they never realized their dreams of a canal.

Independence from Spain

Panama gained independence from Spain in 1821. However, the country joined the confederacy of Gran Colombia, the Latin American countries united by Simon Bolivar. When this alliance later disbanded, Panama remained part of Colombia.

Colombia continued the quest for an interoceanic canal, though a railroad was built first. Constructed in 1855, at the time of the San Francisco gold rush, the 50-mile (80-km) rail route through Panama proved the safest transit for North Americans heading from the East to the West coast.

The French Attempt

The railroad was considered merely a temporary measure, and in 1880 Colombia finally sold the rights to build a canal to the French Compagnie Universelle du Canal Interocéanique. This attempt resulted in tragic failure. Led by Ferdinand de Lesseps, who had successfully engineered the Suez Canal, the French endeavored to construct a similar sea-level canal in Panama. Thick rain forest, intense tropical conditions, and disease defeated the attempt; around 22,000 lives were lost to yellow fever and malaria. The project was abandoned in 1888.

Independence from Colombia and the Panama Canal

Panama's chance for independence came in 1903 when Philippe Bunau-Varilla, who had been an engineer under De Lesseps, devised a way to restore French losses. Instigating the idea of a Panamanian revolution, he offered Washington a bargain price for canal rights in return for U.S. support of Panama's attempt to gain independence from Colombia. Washington agreed. On November 3, 1903, Panama launched its revolt. Colombia was powerless against the threat of U.S. warships, and Panama declared itself an independent republic. It paid a high price for this independence: the treaty signed between U.S. Secretary of State John Hay and Philippe Bunau-Varilla gave the U.S.A. full rights to the construction, protection, and operation of a canal through Panama "in perpetuity," and full and judicial control of a ten-mile-wide zone from ocean to ocean. Consequently, the U.S.A. was able to proceed "as if it were the sovereign of the territory." In addition to independence, Panama received U.S. $10 million for this treaty, and an annual sum of U.S. $250,000.

The Americans constructed a canal above sea level that utilized an exceptional system of lock gates. Workers came mainly from the West Indies, but others arrived from far reaches of the globe, making the construction project a truly multiethnic achievement, and adding further to Panama's multicultural heritage. The canal took ten years to complete, and was a vast improvement on the French effort. Tropical diseases were eradicated, and health care for the workers became a priority. The first boat, the *Ancon*, sailed through the Panama Canal on August 15, 1914; the canal opened just in time for the First World War.

Omar Torrijos and the Military
Repeated U.S. intervention in internal Panamanian affairs produced increasing hostility between the two countries. Attempts to deal with these conflicts began in 1926, but a treaty was not agreed upon until 1939, when Panama's status as a U.S. protectorate was formally terminated. The treaty however, only "relaxed" U.S. intervention rights and made no changes to the canal rights

outlined in the Hay–Bunau-Varilla treaty. Under the name Guardia Nacional, and with U.S. backing, Panama's military began to expand.

From 1903 Panama was a constitutional democracy, but power remained effectively in the hands of a wealthy oligarchy, which perpetuated deep class divisions within the country. Various politicians had attempted to steer governmental policies toward social reforms; Arnulfo Arias Madrid and his "Panameñista" movement was perhaps the best-known. However, in 1968 the leader of the Guardia Nacional, General Omar Torrijos Herrera, deposed the newly elected President Arias and assumed military control over the country. Power was finally removed from the oligarchic elite.

Despite his position as a dictator in Panama, Torrijos became one of the country's favorite leaders. He radically improved racial equality in the country and introduced economic, social, labor, and land reforms to help fight poverty. Further, Torrijos demanded new canal rights, which were finally agreed to in 1977 by U.S. President Jimmy Carter. The new treaty, signed in 1979, ended U.S. control over the Canal, gave Panama full rights from December 31, 1999, and guaranteed the Canal's permanent neutrality. In 1981, Torrijos was killed in a plane crash. To this day rumors abound that the crash was no accident.

Manuel Antonio Noriega

In 1983 Panama's most notorious figure, Manuel Antonio Noriega, took control of the National Guard. Fresh from extreme anticommunist militant training, Noriega, a previous Washington CIA informer, quickly assumed power, renaming his expanding army the Panama Defense Forces (PDF). During the ensuing six years, Noriega created mayhem in Panamanian politics, which not only wreaked economic havoc but also ended in tragedy for some innocent Panamanians (see below). Noriega was long suspected of involvement in extensive drugs and arms trafficking, but his most notable misdemeanor was an alleged connection to the gruesome murder of the former vice health minister and member of the opposition Hugo Spadafora, in 1985. Additionally, he had twice fraudulently interfered with elections in Panama (although the first time he was reportedly backed by the U.S.A.). North America had had enough. Deemed a threat to the security of the canal and wanted on drug smuggling charges, America began efforts to drive out Noriega. Despite a failed military coup against him, in 1989 Noriega overturned the legitimate results of the National Assembly elections. The sitting Assembly gave him full power and elected him head of government in December. America tightened its sanctions, and the country was on the road to economic disaster.

Operation Just Cause
A possible justification for military invasion was found on December 16, when a member of the PDF shot an unarmed U.S. marine soldier in civilian dress. On December 20, 1989, under U.S. President George Bush, America launched Operation Just Cause, maintaining this as necessary to "safeguard the lives of Americans, to defend democracy in Panama, to combat drug trafficking and to protect the integrity of the Panama Canal Treaty." However, the invasion was condemned by the United Nations and the Organization of American States as a violation of international law. The U.S. attacked around 4,000 Panamanian troops with an army numbering 26,000 and dropped over 400 bombs during the first thirteen hours. The U.S. specifically targeted Noriega's offices in El Chorrillo, a poor district of Panama City. The exact Panamanian death toll is unknown, with estimated numbers ranging from several hundred to more than 4,000. The U.S.A. lost twenty-three soldiers.

Noriega emerged from hiding on January 3, 1990, and was later sentenced to forty years in a Florida prison for drug-trafficking offenses.

Readjustment after the War
Panama's military was dissolved in 1990, shortly after Operation Just Cause. The Panamanian Public Forces (PPF) was introduced; this is an organization directly answerable to the civilian authorities that includes the Panamanian National Police, the National Maritime Service, and the National Air Service. The U.S.A., amid Operation Just Cause, reinstated Guillermo Endara, the ousted winner of the 1989 elections, as president. However, he was unable to fulfill either Panamanian or U.S. political hopes. Rumors continued to link the government to drug trafficking, while the country struggled to recover economically, despite the relaxation of U.S. sanctions, and there was ongoing public protest. In 1992 Endara's government held a referendum on a set of constitutional reforms that included the abolition of the army. Panamanians voted against the reforms, although the voter turnout was low. Many saw the result as another mark against Endara's government. Endara finally admitted defeat and in 1994 Ernesto Perez Balladares was elected, returning Panama to Torrijo's Democratic Revolutionary Party.

Relations with the U.S.A. slowly improved, as did the country's economy. Four years after the dissolution of the PDF, the Legislative Assembly passed a constitutional amendment that permanently abolished the Panamanian national army. However, provisional forces are permitted under the amendment in exceptional circumstances, such as foreign hostility. Military expenditure in Panama is around U.S. \$147 million, 1.1 percent of GDP (2004 figures).

Like Endara's, the Balladares government was also accused of corruption, and in 1998 the public voted in a referendum against the extension of his presidential term.

Mireya Moscoso, widow of former President Arnulfo Arias Madrid, won the election in 1999, becoming the country's first female president. Although she pledged to strengthen social programs, there were accusations of corruption and fraud, and many unresolved scandals have been associated with her government.

Canal Handover

At the commencement of the Torrijos treaty, to cover the ensuing phaseout of U.S. control, the Panama Canal Commission was set up as the Canal's official Panamanian governing body. On December 31, 1999, the commission was renamed the Panama Canal Authority (ACP) and the Canal was successfully and formally handed over to Panamanian control. Additionally, Panama took possession of the U.S. military facilities in the former Panama Canal Zone, and the U.S. Southern Command and U.S. Army South troops moved out of the country. Many Panamanians took to the streets with patriotic flags and banners during the handover celebrations, thrilled that now, after almost a hundred years, they had finally achieved complete sovereignty. However, as the U.S. operations associated with the military bases closed down, around 4,000 Panamanians lost their jobs. Panama suffered economic loss both in terms of employment for the U.S. military and in income from U.S. expenditure in the country. But this is now largely forgotten, and the management of the Panama Canal continues to function smoothly.

Panamanian Government Today

There has recently been a feeling of weariness throughout the country regarding politics, and many Panamanians appear tired of the continual struggle to be heard, and of the recurring stories of fraud that surround the government. However, there was an 80 percent turnout for the May 2004 presidential elections, demonstrating the Panamanian commitment to the political process. The PRD (Democratic Revolutionary Party) candidate Martin Torrijos Espino (son of Omar Torrijos), who was defeated by Moscoso in 1999, won the elections by 47 percent of the vote and became president on September 1, 2004. A new feeling of national hope has attended his first year in office, as many Panamanians believe he will improve standards as his father did before him.

The Economy of the Panama Canal

Economically the Canal is Panama's finest asset, and has contributed an average of 6 percent of Panama's GDP since the 1980s. An astonishing 5 percent of world trade transits the Canal, which serves eighty countries and 120 trade routes. According to the Panama Canal Authority (ACP), approximately 13,000 vessels carrying between them roughly 188 million long tons in cargo pass through the waterway annually. Fourteen percent of this trade is U.S. commerce, making America the Canal's largest client. Each year tariffs rise by approximately 2 percent, although 2004-5 saw a higher, twofold, rise. For the 2003 fiscal year the ACP recorded toll revenues reaching U.S. $920.8 million (including money from related canal services); of this U.S. $258 million was the Panama Canal Authority's net income.

THE PANAMA CANAL

To comprehend fully the scale and magnitude of a vessel's transit through the Panama Canal, one needs to witness the process firsthand. Its effectiveness relies on a set of twelve locks, six (three going each way) on either side of the 50-mile (80-km) waterway that stretches from the Pacific to the Atlantic. The locks are vast, measuring 110 feet (33.53 m) wide by 1,050 feet (320 m) long, and 85 feet (25.9 m) deep. However, when an immense Panamax vessel (a ship measuring the maximum size to fit through the locks), laden with cargo, squeezes through the gates, the locks look quite dainty in comparison.

The lock chambers are staggered on each side of the Canal and raise vessels to 85 feet (26 m) above sea level and lower them again at the other end. Towering miter gates secure vessels in the chambers while 43 million gallons (197 million liters) of fresh water are pumped into, or drained out of, each cavity. The water is supplied from Gatún Lake, and is eventually flushed into the sea. Up to eight electric towing locomotives, known as "mules," run on tracks on each side of the locks to help support the vessels' passage. Modern mules are made by Mitsubishi, weigh approximately 55 tons, are able to pull around 311.8 kilonewtons, and cost, on average, U.S. $2 million.

The thinnest stretch of the Canal runs 7.8 miles (12.6 km) from the Pedro Miguel Lock on the Pacific to Gatún Dam, where it crosses the continental divide. Originally named the Culebra Cut, it was renamed the Gailllard Cut after its engineer, Major David du Bose Gaillard, who died two years before the Canal was completed. Excavating it involved hacking through rock 210 feet (64 m) above sea level, which was the hardest part of the Canal's initial construction. Toward the end of the last century the Cut was becoming too narrow for the Canal's two-lane traffic. It was widened in 2001, and this work continues. The number of vessels unable to fit through the Canal (labeled post-Panamax vessels) is rising, and there are plans to increase its width, including building a third lane, currently in process (see below).

The Panama Canal has two bridges— Puente de las Américas (Bridge of the Americas), and the recently constructed Puente Centinario (Centenary Bridge).

Overall, approximately U.S. $150 million is invested each year in the maintenance of the Panama Canal.

The plans to widen the Canal must undergo a rigorous and lengthy scrutiny before they can be approved. There are several types of vessel in use today that cannot squeeze through the locks, and this limits trade. The ACP suggests in its proposals that they pay half the cost of the widening project. The other half would be sourced from private bank loans. This could provide a very lucrative business prospect.

Those who oppose the project suggest that the cost will outweigh the return. The ACP estimates

the finished project at around U.S. $5 billion, but critics calculate that the final costs are more likely to be around U.S. $8 billion. Conservation and environmental concerns are an additional worry, and much remains to be discussed before work starts to update Panama's premier service to the international trade.

THE ECONOMY TODAY
Despite a rocky financial history (in particular during the Noriega years), inflation has remained at a stable and impressive rate of between 1 and 2 percent for the last thirty years. The Panama

Canal, the Colón Free Zone, the international banking sector, and, especially, the use of the U.S. dollar, have secured this steady state. An additional factor is the growing tourist industry. The service economy accounts for approximately 75 percent of GNP, industry 16 percent, and agriculture 10 percent. Major exports include bananas, shrimp, and sugar. Coffee, rice, corn, potatoes, onions, pork, and chicken are also exported in smaller quantities. However, current economic reports show inflation has risen to 3 percent for the first time in twenty-three years. The government has responded rapidly, cutting fuel prices in an attempt to lower costs.

A less rosy aspect of the economy is Panama's unequal distribution of wealth: 37 percent of the population remain below the poverty line (1999) and unemployment at 12.6 percent (2004) is relatively high. Although standards have vastly improved since Noriega's time, poverty levels remain high in a country that holds one of the world's most profitable waterways.

Banking
Panama is almost as famous for its international banks, which have been portrayed in fiction as "laundrettes" for dirty money, as it is for its Canal. In reality, Panama's banking laws have toughened up over recent years and in 1998 were regulated to

meet the Basle Committee's standards for transparency and reporting.

There are now over eighty international banks in Panama, representing more than thirty-two countries. Most attractive to foreigners are Panama's offshore services, offering clients stringent banking secrecy and tax-free laws. The Panama World Trade Center is located in the heart of the banking district.

The Colón Free Zone

Established in 1948, Panama's Colón Free Zone is now the largest in the Western hemisphere, and second-largest in the world. The Free Zone is administered as an autonomous institution of the Panamanian government, and the country now has the highest import and export levels in Latin America. In 2004, it accounted for 92 percent of Panama's exports and 65 percent of its imports.

Within the 988 acres (400 hectares) of the Free Zone there are approximately 1,750 traders, generating around U.S. $11 billion in exports and reexports annually. Around 250,000 visitors visit the Zone each year.

Free Trade Future

While Panama has a number of bilateral free trade agreements with countries worldwide, it has not yet been able to reach an agreement with the

United States. The U.S.–driven Central America Free Trade Agreement (CAFTA), creating the second-largest free trade zone in Latin America, was signed in 2005. However, as Panama is not officially in the Central America trading bloc, its negotiations with the U.S.A. have been independent of CAFTA.

The current government supports free trade with the U.S.A., and it is expected that the Panamanian Assembly will approve an agreement in the future. However, talks about a free trade agreement in January 2006 ended inconclusively and have now been postponed while further investigation is made. Parts of the agricultural sector, unhappy about removing tariffs on certain products,

have expressed their opposition, but it is unlikely that this would be sufficient to overturn a ruling, should one eventually be passed.

Annual trade between Panama and the U.S.A. totals U.S. $1.4 billion, with a U.S. $1 billion advantage. The U.S.A. also has more investments in Panama than the Central American trading bloc combined, worth around U.S. $25 billion.

chapter two

VALUES &
ATTITUDES

THE PANAMANIAN WAY

As we have seen, Panama's global mix of
inhabitants has resulted in a unique blend of
Latin Americanism. There are many similarities
with other Latin Americans, including religious
belief, the importance of the family, and pride, all
of which are strong throughout the region.
However, generations of foreign settlers, such as
West Indians, Chinese, and in particular North
Americans, have brought new flavors, styles, and
even work ethics to this tiny nation.

Panamanian people are friendly, polite, and
relaxed. They are traditionally devout, although in
recent years younger generations have become
more relaxed about churchgoing and observing
religious customs. Many older people still live by
age-old superstitions. For example, they say that
putting a shirt on inside out will keep witches at
bay, and a black cat that crosses your path brings
bad luck (as opposed to the belief in some
countries that it brings good luck). Young people
usually remember their grandparents' old wives'

tales, although they may dismiss them and will never admit to belief in superstitions. This is a small example of Panamanian pride—which is just as characteristic. Panamanians are image-conscious, and those who can afford it, both male and female, dress well, and have the knack of looking elegant in both formal and casual clothes.

Most Panamanians know what it is to be poor. Though they may not have experienced great poverty themselves, it could be a memory that their parents or grandparents have shared with them. They may have some money for shopping or socializing, but generally they do not throw it around. Visitors may find that Panamanians do not always offer to foot a restaurant bill or lavish friends with gifts in the way that some cultures do, and this is usually simply because they can't afford it. However, with the exception of grand displays of foreign wealth, they will not expect others to behave any differently.

Cooperation

Panama is a small country, and most people are accustomed to a communal lifestyle. What visitors may interpret as intrusive or interfering behavior is most likely to be a Panamanian's way of being neighborly, and while Panamanians can sometimes be unfussy and direct, they may simply be trying to help. One wonderful quality is their optimistic approach to overcoming everyday hurdles. If someone has a problem, friends and neighbors are prepared to shoulder the burden and help them. This ranges from offering to fix a car to tackling jobs such as plumbing repairs, and even replacing an entire roof, which foreigners might deem impossible without professional help. This supportive, can-do attitude has given Panamanians great flexibility, the capacity to ignore red tape, and perhaps a less materialistic attitude than more developed cultures are accustomed to. The impression is that many Panamanians would be able to survive long-term if they found themselves lost in the wilderness, which is a comforting feeling.

Politically, however, Panamanians are typically pessimistic. The crisis (and embarrassment) Noriega brought to their country, the U.S. invasion, and a repeated history of governmental corruption have created a generation that almost expects to be let down again. But politics and patriotism are two very different concepts to Panamanians, who remain deeply nationalistic despite a dented political vision.

Looking Good

For a Panamanian city dweller, a smart, groomed appearance is a top priority, and both men and women present themselves flawlessly for all occasions, business or casual. It's essential that clothes, shoes, hair, and makeup are impeccable. Young people are very particular about the "right" designer labels, which can earn instant respect purely because such a label announces wealth. People with money in Panama are noticeable, from the strings of pearls they wear to the Mercedes, BMWs, and other high-performance cars that move grandly around shopping mall forecourts.

In rural areas outside the cities, labels disappear, but the basic law of dressing well persists and you will see men and women going to work in formal suits even on the hottest days. Panamanians cannot understand why a person would not care about their dress in public. Even those hovering near the poverty line dress as smartly as possible just to run to the shops.

Foreigners should know that it is illegal for men to walk in the streets in Panama without a shirt, and the police will approach you if you do so. Churches in particular require visitors to be dressed modestly, and it is advisable to restrict shorts and miniskirts to the beach and beach resorts. Additionally, some Panamanian Indians may take offense at bikinis and skimpy clothes.

GOOD MANNERS

Courtesy is as important to Panamanians as good dress sense. Good manners are particularly applicable with the elderly, who are paid great attention throughout the country. Panamanians can be very laid-back, and are not easily insulted, but usually measure you by your interest in them.

On arrival in any situation, after introductions it is considered civil to inquire after the person's family. Panamanians will usually ask you "Where is your husband (or wife)?" and "How are your mother and father?" even if they have never met your spouse or parents. Such questions are not only considered good etiquette, but arise from a genuine interest in family and status, which are important in their own lives. Panamanians will almost certainly send their *saludas* (health) to your family, and it is polite for you to repay the compliment. Asking further questions about their family, such as what they do, and where they live, is not considered impolite; on the contrary, it shows a genuine interest in their lives.

Something else for those from the U.S.A. to remember is that Panamanians are also American —Latin American. Don't say you come from "America." A Panamanian may rightly answer, "But I, too, am American." You should say that you are from "*Estados Unidos.*"

The Language—Formal and Informal
Panamanians use formal Spanish in conversation with strangers, and even with acquaintances. It is

only between good friends that the formality is relaxed. If you want to meet and converse with Panamanians, it is essential to learn basic formal Spanish, and to understand the difference between the formal and informal modes. It is very easy, for example, to say "*tu*" (informal "you") instead of "*usted*" (formal "you"), and in many circumstances this would be very bad manners. Panamanians are likely to realize that such a lapse from a foreigner is a genuine mistake, and are unlikely to take offense or reprimand you; but it would show greater respect to reflect their good manners and learn the correct usage. Even if you feel more relaxed with a new friend, it is best to stick to formal speech, at least until they use informal speech with you. This way you will never offend a Panamanian.

"*Con permiso*" ("Excuse me") is a good phrase to remember; it is used exactly as English speakers would use it, from passing people in busy crowds to politely interrupting a conversation.

MACHISMO

Machismo remains a rather overlooked problem in Panama. While on the surface it appears to be declining, male dominance is still a powerful factor in Latin culture. Traditionally in Panama it was acceptable for husbands to have (and support) mistresses, and although this is now less commoon, it still happens. Men oddly don't feel much remorse; they feel that since they worship their wives as their *reina* (queen), the minor matter of someone on the side should mean nothing in their major relationship.

Panamanian women today recall that until recently their husbands would not be seen on the street pushing their child's stroller, or even interacting with their baby. This was the mother's role. Now, however, these mind-sets are changing, and in Panama you will see fathers, and even grandfathers, taking an active part in the upbringing of children. Nevertheless, it is still rare for men to wash the dishes or clean the house.

As in other Latin countries, *machismo* has been ingrained in men for generations. Panamanian boys are traditionally raised to be tough, some believing that while they are perhaps not better than women, they are stronger and more competent. Some fathers still take a son to a strip club on his sixteenth birthday, as a "rite of passage," a now dwindling tradition that arguably heightens feelings of male dominance.

Women visiting Panama, however, are likely to witness only minor levels of *machismo*: whistles, and comments such as "*Guapa*" (good looking), "*Bonita*" (pretty), and "*Hermosa*" (beautiful), are commonly directed by men at passing women.

These are harmless compliments, and usually mean nothing more. Don't bat an eyelid!

RACIAL ATTITUDES

There is much casual racism in Panama, which has a vast cultural mix. Historically, black people have had to fight for equal rights, and the days of the Canal construction saw disgraceful inequalities, such as whites being paid with gold and blacks with silver. Things have, of course, progressed; Torrijos was a major force in initiating racial equality.

Today, racism is still evident in everyday behavior and speech. *Mestizo* Panamanians frequently use nicknames according to race. For example, they will refer to any person of Asian descent as "*Chino*" (masculine) or "*China*" (feminine), and to a person of West Indian descent as "*Negro*." Many *mestizos* can't see a problem with this, and the habit is so common that most of those on the receiving end show no sign of being in the slightest way offended or affected. But some, mainly blacks, who have long felt the weight of racism, are more sensitive.

"SHORT-TERMISM"

The majority of Panamanians have had some experience of economic hardship, some far greater than others. Many live today with an inner fear of what may happen tomorrow, and this is especially true, of course, in deprived areas. Therefore many Panamanians believe it is best to take what they can get while it is there, preferring to have a stable job with a modest, regular income, rather than to embark on a speculative enterprise with possible good prospects.

A good example of this "short-termism" is the ongoing debate over marine turtles, of which large numbers visit Panama each year to lay eggs on the beaches. Stories are told of a time when fishermen could not maneuver their boats ashore because of the quantity of turtles on the beach. The turtles traditionally provided meat and shells for local food and trade, but in the last fifty years their numbers have declined drastically, because of extensive hunting (mainly for tourists) and fishing practices throughout the world, and their extinction in the near future is predicted. Numerous conservation groups have voiced their concern, but some people continue to poach them. When tackled about this, they reply that they and their children are starving today, so they cannot think about possible extinction tomorrow. While the loss of the relatively few turtles killed by individuals to feed their families is not likely to affect the situation, the large numbers killed for the black market will.

This argument could also explain the rate of deforestation, which, although currently providing good local employment, holds out the worry of a future for Panama without its precious rain forest resources.

CLASS SYSTEMS

What is perhaps most immediately striking about Panama City is the major class divide. Wealth is paraded in glittering, high-rise, luxury blocks just streets away from shantytowns. On a short walk you can observe affluent, beautifully dressed men and women, the latter parading pearls and diamonds, and also ragged, impoverished, and homeless people. The city of Colón is in a severe state of economic depression, and yet in the same vicinity, with simply a wall to contain it, the Colón Free Zone is possibly Panama's second most lucrative economic asset.

Less obvious is the class system within the country as a whole. Most of Panama's wealth is located around the three major cities and some high-class beach resorts. These areas are a sharp contrast to rural areas, many of which are off the beaten path, where poor people still live in very basic conditions and rely on modest crops for survival. Panama has a history of deeply unequal income distribution, and in 1994 was rated below

Brazil, the bottom 20 percent of the population receiving just 2 percent of national income while the top 5 percent received 18 percent.

PROTEST AND DISSENT

Throughout the country's history, Panamanians have taken to the streets to fight their causes, sometimes with exceptionally good reasons.

The Day of the Martyrs is celebrated in memory of twenty-one Panamanians killed and 400 wounded by U.S. soldiers during the "Flag Demonstrations," a student protest in 1964 against the U.S. refusal to raise a Panamanian flag alongside the American flag outside a Canal Zone high school in Balboa. Young students who died amid the protests included Estanislao Orobio, a seventeen-year-old who was shot as he walked on Canal Zone turf with the Panamanian flag, and Ascanio Arosemena, a student not involved in the protests, who simply stopped to help another victim. A shrine now stands outside the high school and the Fourth of July Avenue was renamed Avenida de los Martires.

Historically it is city students who have initiated protests, and who still continually lobby the government for social reforms, including improved educational opportunities for the rural poor. Recent protests include street riots against the 2001 rise in Panama City bus fares from fifteen to twenty-five cents, which infuriated locals whose wages did not see a similar rise, and President Mireya Moscoso's authorization of what amounted to millions spent on the Miss Universe 2003 competition at the newly inaugurated Figali Convention Center in Panama City. Moscoso believed it was important for Panama's tourist economy, and a part of their centennial celebrations; many others believed the money would have been better spent on the declining social services.

ATTITUDES TO THE U.S.A.

Its previous ownership of the Panama Canal meant that the U.S.A. dominated almost a hundred years of Panamanian history. Not surprisingly, this long episode has left its mark.

There is now a general divide in attitudes toward the U.S.A. A large number of working- and middle-class Panamanians were sorry to see the U.S.A.'s departure from Panama in 1999, and still believe that the employment situation was better under its management. Undeniably, the U.S.A. (along with the Spanish and the French) helped to introduce the tiny isthmus of Panama to the global marketplace. However, academics, the political left, and many middle-class circles were delighted to see Panamanian control established at last over their most important asset. Many Panamanians still feel bruised and skeptical over repeated U.S. interventions throughout preceding years, and the scars of Noriega and Operation Just Cause are still felt by all. However, in the main, Panamanians have a relatively pro-American stance, and you will find little, if any, discrimination against American people.

The Kuna Indians, as we have seen, have a special, positive relationship with North America that continues to this day.

ATTITUDES TO FOREIGNERS

Attitudes to foreigners have changed greatly in recent years. Although Panama has seen countless foreign visitors, many arrived solely for business reasons. Relations with native Panamanians have not been a high priority.

During the last century, American citizens working for the Panama Canal were isolated within the Canal Zone, which provided high schools, shopping malls, and health services, so that they never needed to enter into Panamanian society. This only hindered U.S.–Panama relations and gave rise to frustration and resentment among Panamanians who felt that America had no interest in them.

Now, however, with the Canal under Panamanian sovereignty, business accountability and relations have shifted completely. Panamanians are in control and finally have a chance to show off their country and all its assets, and are welcoming the integration of foreign arrivals. Additionally, the influx of expatriates and retired people means more business and more employment on Panamanian terms. Foreigners are moving to the country not simply because of Panama's beauty, but specifically because Panamanian people have a reputation for welcoming foreigners.

Relations are becoming better balanced, especially in terms of foreign residents learning Spanish. Tourism is still relatively new, and locals find tourists quite a novelty. Panamanians are learning to reap the benefits of tourism and are genuinely thrilled that their country has at last been put on the map in such a positive manner, after so many years of negative press.

CUSTOMS & TRADITIONS

RELIGION

Catholicism is deeply rooted in Panama, where the Catholic Church embraces around 86 percent of the population. It was introduced in the early sixteenth century by the Spanish, who settled in

the Darién region and founded Santa María la Antigua del Darién, which became the first diocese to be recognized in the New World. Today, many old church and cathedral ruins are scattered throughout the country, the oldest in Natá, in the province of Cocles.

Rural Panamanians are deeply religious. This is evident in their everyday life, in their speech, prayers, and folklore, and in the small shrines that adorn the corners of their houses. City dwellers likewise retain a strong attachment to the faith, but the numbers regularly attending church are much lower. Whether they attend church regularly or not, most Panamanians demonstrate a religious cast of mind in their everyday dealings. For example you will frequently hear them whispering "*Gracias a Dios*" ("Thanks be to God") after statements such as, "My journey here was easy," or comments about the good health of their children. Panamanians will cross themselves, speak openly about asking God for help, and show gratitude for a particular run of luck. This seems to reflect genuine belief rather than just habitual usage, and extends across generations and classes, and from family life to business. People seem to hold God responsible for everything, no matter how trivial. Furthermore, historically, the Church has played a strong political role in Panama, and both right- and left-wing parties have used religious authority to endorse their political stratagems.

Protestant Christianity was introduced in the early nineteenth century and now accounts for approximately 8 percent of Panamanians, with Methodism established as the main branch.

Missionaries have repeatedly attempted to enter Panama's native communities, and continue to do so today. While some are living amicably within Indian communities, and presumably having some effect on their lives, others have not been accepted. Reportedly Ngöbe Buglé people recently asked missionaries to leave them in peace. It is widely accepted that the impact of the missionaries will affect the future of Panama's native Indians.

MODERN FAITH v. *FIESTEROS*

The "*fiesta* spirit" of Panamanians has begun to worry the Church, which feels that the usual celebratory practices of drinking and partying after traditional ceremonies are eclipsing the events' religious significance.

Religious holidays and festivals in Panama have long been accompanied by dancing and merriment. Los Carnavales (see page 62), for example, is known for its riotous street events. These involve massive water hoses and "shaving foam fights" that go hand-in-hand with high intakes of alcohol and inebriety. More and more young groups take to the streets with coolers of beer, and will often stay out and "party"  for the entire four days of the Carnaval. Partygoers in Panama have been nicknamed "*fiesteros*," but the name is normally applied to those who continually stay out late and drink more than average, rather than those who party on odd occasions. It is not only the Church that worries over *fiesteros*; the government also has its concerns. It is usual for the sale of alcohol to be prohibited on the day of a general election, to ensure that *fiesteros* do not start early enough to interfere with polling.

That said, patron saints' days are of major significance to Panamanian families, and religious education, though not obligatory, is important to them. Any Panamanian can explain the meaning of the religious date at hand—however drunk he or she may be!

FIESTAS

Panamanians work hard, and a good *fiesta* (party) is a favorite way to relax. Music, dancing, and socializing are long-established Panamanian essentials, and the enthusiasm can be infectious to visitors. From family get-togethers to large communal street events, Panamanians throw some of the best parties in Latin America.

Family parties are held on the occasions of christenings, birthdays, engagements, and weddings, and may be celebrated at home, or in a bar or a function room. They are usually exclusive to family members and very close friends.

Girls traditionally celebrate their fifteenth birthdays with a large gathering of friends, often in a rented hotel room, and many young people first learn to dance salsa and merengue style specifically for one of these events. Fifteenth birthday parties are sophisticated, and are usually the first formal event for young people. Girls wear gowns and ball dresses, boys black tie. Fifteen is just the starting age, and you will find all generations, including the grandparents, joining in the revelry. Panamanians' collective love of *fiesta* is obvious, and they will often find any excuse, or even invent a reason, to throw a party.

FESTIVALS AND HOLIDAYS

Festivals and *ferias* (fairs) are often spectacular events, and there are a large number of them throughout the year. Each province in Panama annually celebrates the day, or days, of its own patron saint, but there are many other celebrations, both religious and nonreligious.

Festivities bring together whole towns and communities, often including people from other provinces, and can take place over a number of days. Most notably, costume and dance have become characteristic features of Panamanian culture. Months are spent working on elaborate masks and outfits that each year seem to try to outdo those of the last. Celebrations include communal street events, colorful processions with floats depicting stories and characters, ceremonial fires, music, and festival "queens." Many events cater to children in the daytime, with family shows and competitions, with the evening given over to music and dancing for the adults.

During most of these festivals no one goes to work, so don't expect to find businesses, shops, or offices open during many holidays, in particular Carnaval, Holy Week, and "patriot week," the first week in November.

NATIONAL HOLIDAYS	
January 1	New Year's Day
January 9	Martyrs' Day
February/March	Los Carnavales (Mardi Gras)
March/April	Good Friday (Viernes Santo)
Mayo 1	Labor Day
November 1	National Anthem Day and Day of the Children
November 2	All Souls' Day
November 3	Independence Day (from Colombia)
November 4	National Flag Day
November 10	First Cry of Independence (from Spain) in Los Santos
November 28	Independence Day (from Spain)
December 8	Immaculate Conception/ Mother's Day
December 25	Christmas Day

NATIONAL DRESS

Panama's national female dress is called the *pollera*. Its design came from sixteenth-century, flamenco-style, Spanish everyday dress, and today is one of the most costly national dresses in the world. The *pollera* has retained the layered frills extending from the bodice to the full length of the skirt, which contains enough material for the wearer to hold out each side without revealing any part of her body underneath. The headpiece, or *tembleque*, was originally made with fish scales and flowers, but now consists of thousands of tiny pearls, beads, and corals, and is further adorned with silky ribbons and gold filigree brooches. The outfit is complemented with gold necklaces and pins, and some of the most spectacular costumes to be seen are those ornamented solely by antique jewelry. These dresses are now vastly expensive —the more intricate the higher the price—and those with antique adornments can fetch thousands of dollars. They are traditionally handed down within the family, however.

The *pollera* is used for traditional dance and provincial festivals, where a woman dancing will gently sway and twirl her skirt. Panamanians believe it to be the ultimate feminine garment; its many frills perfectly flatter a woman's shape. The dress is celebrated annually on July 22 in Los Santos. An additional event, named "The Thousand Pollera Parade," has recently been created in Panama City and is held in June.

The Panamanian traditional dress for men is much simpler. It consists of a white cotton shirt and trousers and a woven straw hat, usually with brown bands around the rim, the number of bands signifying the origin within the country.

THE FESTIVE CALENDAR
January 1: New Year's Day
New Year's Day is chiefly a family occasion, with a church service and family meals.

January 6: Dia De Reyes Magos
Epiphany is not a national holiday, but children receive small gifts, and this day is generally recognized as the end of the Christmas period.

January 9: Martyrs' Day
Martyrs' Day commemorates twenty-one Panamanians killed by U.S. soldiers in the 1964 student riots resulting from the refusal of the U.S.A. to allow the Panamanian flag to be flown in a high school within the Canal Zone. This is a day

of respect, rather than a *fiesta*. (See Protest and Dissent, in Chapter 2).

February/March: Los Carnavales
Locals will argue that the famous Latin festival of Mardi Gras is as greatly anticipated by Panamanians in Panama as it is by Brazilians in Rio. Not surprisingly, Panama's celebrations are on a smaller scale; but anyone experiencing the Carnaval in Panama cannot argue with the country's devotion to the event.

Celebrated during the four days preceding Ash Wednesday, the party simply does not stop. Traditionally, the town is split into two groups, or *tunas*, reflecting the socioeconomic divide. *Calle Arriba* represents the wealthy part of town, and *Calle Abajo* the poorer. Over the four days, the sides compete in various events and competitions. Each *tuna* has a beautiful female representative, and the winner is crowned Queen.

The Carnaval requires a sense of fun, and those willing to get involved will not forget the experience. It can take an entire year to prepare and build the floats, and costumes are often incredibly intricate. Traditional headdresses alone are spectacular, swathed with sequins and colored feathers. The festivities have become bold and sometimes outrageous, and the sights can be spectacular. Streets pulsate with both live music and

salsa and reggaeton (a mix of rap and reggae) from mountains of speakers hired for the event. People arrive with blue dye and shaving cream for the now very popular foam fights, and helpful attendants with fire engines and huge tankers of water happily keep those dancing on the street cool. Floats and parades appear at night, when the atmosphere seems calmer—although people are just preparing for late-night parties!

The best-known and most typically Panamanian Carnaval is celebrated in Los Santos, where thousands of people congregate in the hot, dusty streets of Las Tablas. Panama City hosts the largest show, with extensive floats and parades. Other provinces have smaller Carnavals, including Penonomé (Coclé), Chitré (Herrera), Chorrera (Panama), and Isla Colón (Bocas del Toro).

March/April: Good Friday (Viernes Santo)
Apart from Christmas, Easter (Semana Santa) is the most important religious celebration of the year. Church services are held on Thursday, Good Friday, and Saturday, and in the evenings there are festivities and dancing. Most of the community will attend Easter celebrations in provincial and rural areas. Easter Sunday's start with morning

mass and Church celebrations can include street processions and reenactments of the Passion.

May 1: Labor Day
This is a national holiday in Panama.

November 1: National Anthem Day and Day of the Children
November is Panama's most patriotic month, with a string of national holidays celebrating the country, independence, and freedom. November 1 begins with festivities for children.

November 2: All Souls' Day
Although this is a declining tradition, some Panamanians still visit the tombs and graves of family members and friends, and simple gatherings are held in their memory.

November 3: Independence Day (from Colombia)
This is one of the most important days in Panama's history, and celebrations are widespread. Towns, houses, and apartment and office blocks are festooned with the red, white, and blue colors of Panama's flag. The day starts with the service of Morning Prayer, after which processions, musical parades, bull running (bloodless, in rural areas), fairs, competitions, and

family events take place throughout the entire country. All Panamanians celebrate. Across Panama various community groups have formed brass bands and these, alongside teams of baton-twirling girls are usually the major attraction of a procession. *Bomberos* (firefighters), many of whom are voluntary, traditionally have a brass band, and can be seen and heard throughout the year practicing in the fire stations.

November 4: National Flag Day

Festivities resume from the previous day. Processions are marked with *banderas* (flags), and show reenactments of Panama's struggle for independence. Students also take the opportunity to bring their protests to the street, peacefully, in the hope that the President will take note. The bands continue to march and play patriotic music. Parades continue into the afternoon, and the evening will see fireworks displays.

November 10: First Cry of Independence (from Spain) in Los Santos

Los Santos celebrates events that are believed to have preceded the country's independence from Spain, which came on November 28, 1821. Although there are no formal records of what occurred, the people of Los Santos believe that events were initiated by a young revolutionary,

Rufina Alfaro. However, many myths and tales surround the story, and the truth is unknown. Festivities abound each year, nonetheless, with folkloric dances and costume and processions.

November 28: Independence Day (from Spain)
Visitors often ask which Independence Day is the more important in Panama—that from Spain or Colombia. Any Panamanian will tell you that both are important, and that both warrant a grand *fiesta*. Hence, the many patriotic festivities similar to those of November 3.

December 8: Immaculate Conception, or Mother's Day
Mother's Day is extremely important to Panamanians, and children never forget it. Mothers are taken for family lunches or dinners, and lavished with flowers. Lucky mamas are even serenaded at midnight.

December 25: Christmas Day
Advent (Adviento) celebrations take place throughout December and each Sunday special prayers are whispered to the *Corona de Adviento*. This, the Advent Crown, is an ornate, usually green candelabrum that holds four candles—

three purple and one pink. One candle is lit each week; the pink candle is the last to be lit, and represents the life of Christ.

A major Christmas parade takes place in Panama City in mid-December with elaborate floats and fairy-tale characters. The parade is a family event and centers on Santa, gifts, and children's entertainment. Parades on a much smaller scale take place across the country, with brass bands and children in fancy dress.

Christmas Eve is celebrated at midnight. Church Mass is first, and the parties begin after the service. Christmas Day is predominantly a family day, with dinners and gatherings mainly at home. Festive foods include turkey, pork, *tamales*, fruitcake, and punch.

LOCAL FESTIVALS AND *FERIAS*
Celebrations vary widely from province to province, from the African Congo dances of Colón to the Spanish-influenced folkloric processions of western provinces. Events celebrate patron saints and historic dates, and different aspects of Panama's culture. The provinces of Herrera and Los Santos in the Azuero peninsula have perhaps more annual celebrations than any other, and their cultural heritage is of paramount importance to local people. Los Carnavales in Las

Tablas is renowned throughout the country. Festivals in the Azuero are taken seriously and some of the most detailed and vibrantly painted masks and costumes can be found there. There are also numerous smaller provincial fairs, or *ferias*, that can be musical, agricultural, or simply a communal celebration. The number of festivals is great, and dates may vary from year to year according to the religious calendar. Listed below are some of the country's major festivities.

January: Feria de las Flores y el Café, Boquete, Chiriquí

This ten-day international flower and coffee fair has become extremely popular, not least because the highland valley town of Boquete is festooned with richly colored flowers growing almost all year-round. Most of Panama's coffee is also grown in this region, and the fair pulls together the stimulating and glorious smells and colors of coffee and flowers. The fair, which has been running for thirty-three years, attracts visitors, including many foreigners, in their thousands.

January/February: Fiesta de los Congos, Portobelo, Colón

Panama's largest black communities live along the Caribbean from the province of Bocas del Toro, but mainly in the province of Colón. Black culture in Panama goes back both to the arrival of West Indian immigrants in the early twentieth century to work on the Canal's construction and in the banana trade, and to slaves from African and Caribbean countries, brought by the Spanish *conquistadores* during and after the sixteenth century. Some of these slaves managed to escape and developed self-sufficient communities deep in the jungle. They became known as Cimarrones, and their history is an integral part of the festival.

The Congo Festival in Portobelo celebrates the mix of African and Catholic heritage in Panama. Locals perform costumed dance, music, congo drumming, and reenactments of slaves escaping from the Spanish, in the apt setting of the ruins of Fort San Geronimo (constructed in 1753), among the surviving cast-iron colonial artillery.

The most renowned dances involve *El Diablo* (the devil) and the *diablitos* (little devils) who are traditionally dressed in red and black with large, elaborate masks decorated with horns and peaks, and usually open-mouthed. The dances represent the battle between good and evil, and the finale sees the slaves saved by the Congo Queen. During the main event, slaves and devils chase and hide throughout the town. *Diablitos* often get carried away, and love to jump out and scare visitors.

The events are a colorful and impressive reminder of a culture sometimes overlooked in

Panama. In particular, you can find Cimarrón art displays and cultural workshops that stand in great contrast to other ethnic events in Panama.

Easter Sunday: Quema de Judas (Burning of Judas), Guararé, Los Santos

This is not an official Church festivity, but one that stems from Panama's country heartlands. After morning Mass a model of Judas, loaded with fireworks, is paraded around the main square, and shortly after set alight. The routine is not merely for religious remembrance but to draw the community together and face up to the year's problems. After the burning of Judas, the *campesinos* (country people) gather in the square and enact mock grief for his death. Judas's "will" is read, which is a list of the various errors committed by individuals in the community throughout the previous year. This can be embarrassing for some, but ultimately unites the villagers in a resolve to forget the problems of the last year and to look forward to a good coming year. Musicians come from across the province, with accordions, guitars, and singing.

July: Festival de la Pollera, Las Tablas, Los Santos

Panama's national dress, the *pollera*, is celebrated during festivities for Santa Librada (the local patron saint), and both are important celebrations

for the province. As well as a parade of dancers in
polleras, there are bullfights, cockfights, dancing,
popular competitions, and religious activities.

August 15: Foundation of Panama City
An official holiday celebrating the foundation
of Panama's capital, Panamá Vieja, which was
completed on August 15, 1519. Panamá Vieja was
dedicated to "Our Lady of the Assumption of
Panama." Events are held within the ruins, where
a stage has recently been built for dramas and
musicals. These tend to be exclusive, however,
being largely attended by the paying middle class.

September: Feria del Mar, Bocas del Toro
This is a lively local festival, celebrating a range
of sounds from folk music and dance to Latin
reggaeton. It takes place by the beach on Isla
Colón in the Bocas del Toro Archipelago.
Although relatively small, it advertises itself as an
international festival, as it has acquired quite a
reputation over preceding years and people come
from neighboring countries especially to attend it.

**September 24: Mejorana Festival, Guararé,
Los Santos,**
In honor of our Lady of Mercedes, the festival has
been celebrated since 1949 and is now considered
one of the most important folkloric festivals in the

country. A procession of painted wagons is typical in the parade, as are music and singing contests.

October 21: Pilgrimage of the Black Christ, Portobelo, Colón

Like the Congo festival, this occasion takes place in Colón and similarly evokes the age of pirates and colonial drama. The pilgrimage and worship of Portobelo's "Cristo Negro," or Black Christ, is the most significant religious annual event in Panama.

The mystery of the arrival of the eight-foot statue remains to this day, although there are various legends. Most agree that the figure was carved in Spain and taken to Panama by ship in the mid-seventeenth century; 1658 has been pinpointed. One story describes a ship unable to leave the docks of Portobelo because of a terrible storm. A number of wooden crates were thrown overboard to lighten the load. Fishermen later discovered the figure inside one of the crates. Another tale claims that the figure was ordered by the people of Taboga Island, on the Pacific side of Panama, but Spain sent the statue in error to Portobelo; numerous attempts to send it to Taboga failed, and the statue became a permanent fixture for Portobelo. Whatever the truth, all Colón locals agree that this figure of Christ did not want to leave the area, and that divine providence kept it where it was.

The Black Christ, also known as the Saint, or the Nazarene, is kept behind a glass altar in the church of San Felipe, and each year is visited by hundreds of pilgrims from Panama and elsewhere. Pilgrims show their devotion to Christ and repent their sins. They may tell him their inner wishes and needs. Many walk for miles to reach Portobelo, some crawling on hands and knees in order to prove their faith.

Traditionally, pilgrims whisper their remorse and pray for miracles as they journey to the site. Purple robes are worn and later cast off on the church steps on their arrival. Mass begins at 6:00 p.m., when the church is full to capacity, with people spilling out of the doors. A four-hour procession begins at 8:00 p.m. when the Black Christ is taken slowly through the town. Despite the gravity of the occasion, there is a festive atmosphere, and those hauling the figure do so with almost dancelike steps.

Visitors may visit the Black Christ throughout the year in the church, and there is a small museum on-site. The statue has a haunting face, and is customarily adorned with luxurious velvet robes, heavy embroidery, and jewels. There is a long history attached to the robes, which are made each year by women in the local community, and displayed in the museum.

chapter four

MAKING FRIENDS

FRIENDS AND ACQUAINTANCES

Panamanians are extremely social, and adore getting together, whether for a chat in the park or for a *fiesta*. That said, social engagements outside the home usually involve large groups of acquaintances, rather than good friends. While it is common for Panamanians to chat at length with acquaintances during parties or communal get-togethers, it is very unlikely that these acquaintances will be invited to their homes or involved in family occasions.

It takes time to become good friends. Such friendships are usually formed at school, at college, or through the family, and it is those relationships that are most valued and lasting.

Dividing lines between friends and acquaintances can become confusing, as Panamanians tend to be so relaxed and friendly on social occasions that they appear to be in an extremely close-knit group. However, they don't generally mix family and close friends with casual friends and acquaintances, and there are some unspoken boundaries between the two. For example, a Panamanian would not suggest that a group of casual friends drop by a family get-together, nor would they invite themselves. They would always wait to be invited to someone's house, and never presume on an acquaintance. Even if you are simply picking someone up from their home, you should not go through the door unless you are invited to do so. If you do overstep the mark, a Panamanian would probably not wish to appear inhospitable, but might become rather standoffish or silent.

Additionally, although Panamanians are accustomed to meeting new people, and indeed thrive on it, they have also seen many foreign visitors come and go, benefiting from employment and resources, and occasionally telling them what to do. Hence, while Panamanians are always keen to make friends and socialize, staying power is tested, and this is another reason why it takes time to progress from casual acquaintance to good friend.

There is a common joke that if you meet one person in Panama, you will know everyone in the country before the week is out. Panama City itself has a surprisingly small-town community atmosphere. People tend to know others in their generation or work area, so most young people in the city seem to know most other young people on the scene, while businesspeople circulate socially with other businesspeople.

So making good friends in Panama takes time, as one would expect in any country. However, given that Panamanians are exceptionally sociable, simply meeting for coffee, or going out for drinks or to the cinema, is not only acceptable and normal, but will be expected. Most Panamanians rate those with the broadest social life as the people most worth knowing. Becoming a social butterfly will raise your local reputation!

If you do become good friends with a Panamanian, you will remain so for life, even if you rarely meet.

LEARNING SPANISH

Although many educated Panamanians, particularly in Panama City, speak English, the majority do not, and so speaking at least basic Spanish is imperative for the visitor who wants to get to know the Panamanians. Learning the language is the easiest way of ensuring that initial meetings will get past general everyday civilities.

There are numerous language programs in Panama City, from introductory to higher, and intensive courses have long been addressing the needs of Americans and foreign business professionals. There are also some well-regarded Spanish schools outside Panama City. Of course, attending language classes is a great way to widen your circle of non-Panamanian friends.

WHERE TO MEET THE PANAMANIANS

Panamanians are very relaxed and easy to talk to, and often socialize in groups; you are very likely to meet people in typical social situations, such as bars, clubs, or community events. In the city, Panamanians prefer to meet friends and acquaintances for coffee, snacks, or drinks, rather than for dinner. In small towns there are often very strong communal ties, and anyone wishing to help or promote the community is usually heartily welcomed into these circles.

The conversations you are likely to have with new Panamanian acquaintances are lighthearted, friendly, and non-taxing. Good topics are family and country. However, surprisingly to many foreigners, political conversations can be welcome, as many Panamanians have an opinion they wish to air. However, while they may enjoy arguing the pros and cons of Panamanian politics, they will not welcome very negative remarks about their country, and political talk should remain tactful and diplomatic. At the end of the night, you should be prepared to have a go at dancing, as this remains a social favorite and always relaxes any tensions!

Young Friends

Young people in Panama use very specific informal lingo between good friends, who can be referred to as *pana* (good friend), *mopri* (Spanish *primo*, cousin, divided and switched around), and *cholo* (mate, specifically masculine). Also, there are not many doorbells in Panama, and young friends stopping by will often whistle from the street or shout "*Hey cholo*" at the window.

PANAMANIAN HOSPITALITY

It is a great honor to be invited to a Panamanian's home for drinks or coffee, and any refusal of such an invitation will be met with surprise. Note that whereas Panamanians themselves are traditionally late, as a visitor it is much better to arrive on time. Being late is something the Panamanians expect from other Panamanians, but not from foreign visitors. Bringing a small gift, such as flowers, wine, or chocolates to a social gathering in the home, is advised as not only will it please the host, but it will show your appreciation and often melt the ice. Panamanians will be particularly pleased with a present from a visitor's home country that is unlike anything available in Panama.

As a guest you will probably be treated very politely. Offers to help, such as by carrying dishes, will be refused. Don't push or insist, as your hosts may feel it is a mark against their hospitality.

NEIGHBORS

Neighbors in the city differ from those in the country only in that it takes longer to get to know them. Other than that, it remains true that Panamanian people enjoy, interact with, and usually know all about those around them. In the city it generally takes longer to get to know your neighbors because high-rise apartment blocks house so many people, and because family houses are spread out. But once established, neighbors often become good acquaintances and while not always becoming good friends, there is an unspoken understanding that they will help each other out when necessary. Neighboring families like to discuss schools and education and exchange local gossip, and the community, however large, continues to develop ties.

CLUBS

Panamanians like clubs and enjoy community events. Apart from the usual council committee meetings and church get-togethers, it is common to find clubs for those with special interests such as music, sports, and various hobbies. Neighborhood bingo games are very popular. In rural areas Panamanians, from children to grandparents, congregate in local parks to play bingo. All are welcome at these local events.

Panama's most famous club is the Union Club. Founded in the early twentieth century, it began as a social club for Panama's oligarchy and the elite in the country. Traditionally, business transactions and negotiations took place over drinks. The club continues today, but it appears to have lost its edge and is generally considered old-fashioned. Nevertheless, while membership is traditionally handed down through generations, the fees are staggeringly high.

Additionally, the Union Club can be fairly restrictive to foreigners, no matter what your rank and status. The shell of what was once one of its most prestigious establishments lies, long disused, in Panama City's colonial quarter, Casco Viejo. Visitors can imagine the elegance this old building once had, with its swimming pool, and its long bar in the main room overlooking the Pacific Ocean.

SOCIALIZING WITH COLLEAGUES

Socializing with business contacts is common in Panama, and regular associates may meet for early evening drinks, either to discuss work or just to relax. If you are a foreigner doing business in Panama it is not unusual for a contact to invite you out—perhaps to bring up some business topic, or impress you, or simply because they are concerned that you may be lonely or feel unwelcome.

Bars are usually the chosen meeting spot, and occasionally casinos. It is common for Panamanians to take visitors around and show them their local area. In Panama City there are numerous restaurants and bars with fine city views, and visitors should take advantage of offers from Panamanian business colleagues to observe the city's best assets. The same applies to other areas of the country: those who work in the area will always know the best and sometimes hidden spots to see. Male visitors should be aware that they might be taken to a strip club as a matter of course, without prior warning.

SOCIALIZING WITH THE OPPOSITE SEX

Socializing with the opposite sex, in business and everyday social circles, is entirely normal, but care should be taken. Male visitors should be aware that Panamanian men can be particularly possessive, and are unlikely to look kindly on another man who tries to strike up a conversation with their wives or girlfriends in a bar or club. Likewise, a single girl may feel you are approaching her with sex in mind rather than with solely platonic intentions. In bars and clubs, men will almost certainly interpret an approach from a woman alone as a come-on. It is more usual to meet the opposite sex by socializing in groups, or through introductions.

EXPATRIATE ASSOCIATIONS AND SPORTS CLUBS

Embassies or consulates and Web sites can provide details of expatriate clubs and organizations in the country. The main expatriate communities in Panama are in the city, Boquete (central highlands), and Bocas del Toro, the three most popular locations.

Internet sites and forums have been created to link up expatriates, and for those thinking of moving to Panama. Some useful firsthand information can be found here, ranging from recommendations on health care and education to how to ship the family dog into the country.

There are a variety of well-endowed golfing clubs in Panama City, as well as health clubs, which usually provide tennis and squash courts, swimming pools, gyms, and spas. These places attract expatriates and wealthy Panamanians, and can provide an excellent setting to meet like-minded people. However, getting involved in the community and taking part in neighborhood events are the best ways of immersing yourself in local culture.

Sportfishing and sailing are extremely popular around Panama, although are mainly now run by expatriates themselves. Seek out a Panamanian-managed business, and the experience will be far more authentic and rewarding. See local marinas for information. There are extensive marinas and sailing clubs located in both Panama City and Colón, at either end of the Panama Canal.

chapter five

THE PANAMANIANS AT HOME

THE FAMILY

Family loyalty is as strong as ever in Panama. The tradition is embedded throughout society, from the tightly held communal beliefs of indigenous people to the members of the twentieth-century oligarchy. In all classes the reflex response, when challenged, is to protect their parents' honor, and to insult someone's mother is unforgivable.

In the first half of the twentieth century, politics in Panama were largely dictated by a wealthy group, including landowners but predominantly from the Canal's commercial and service sector, with deep-rooted family ties. Labeled the *rabiblancos* (white tails, a derogatory term), they were disbanded after Omar Torrijos and the military took over in 1968. It is evident now, just by looking at street names in Panama City, that these families were integral to Panamanian history. Many Panamanians today have distant ties to this infamous oligarchy in their family tree, which is perhaps one cause of family loyalty today.

If you have family connections in Panama, no matter how distant, you will be welcomed into your relatives' homes, even though they might never have met you before. Family connections are strong in the area of business, too. The dentist recommended by your friend may turn out to be his cousin's brother-in-law.

Traditionally, family numbers were large, but this has changed over recent decades, especially within urban areas, where couples are choosing to have fewer children. Larger families are still fairly common in poor rural areas, where it is felt that the more children they have, the  more hands to work, and the greater the future income. Additionally, in both rural and city areas it is usual for offspring to stay in the family home until they get married, for economic reasons.

Most wealthy Panamanians have staff to help in the home; these may include a nanny, a cook, and a cleaner. However, in urban areas and throughout the country, working and middle-class mothers now face similar dilemmas to those in other countries who are trying to juggle paid work, child care, and housekeeping. Customarily, fathers were the breadwinners while mothers stayed at home with the children. Now, it has been a rise in living costs rather than a desire for a career that has caused many mothers to go out to work as well as fathers. Very often grandmothers take turns with child care, and many young people today view their grandmothers in a similar light to their mothers.

Despite this, mothers are still doted on, and Mother's Day is taken very seriously in Panama. Although the tradition is declining, especially in cities, it is still common for Panamanian  men to organize musicians to serenade their wives. This happens on both Mother's Day and Valentine's Day, usually on the stroke of midnight, and is seen as a romantic and honorable gesture.

Children

The youngest family members are typically adored in Panama, and proud parents love to dress up their children. You will see girls wearing pretty lace and satin dresses with ribbons in their hair and shiny shoes, and boys in formal shirts and little ties for church and special occasions.

Babies are welcomed and treasured. They are usually baptized, and the event is celebrated with a family party. Also, babies are traditionally given a red beaded bracelet to wear, from birth, which is thought to protect them from illness and bring them luck. This is still a common custom, and many Panamanians insist on the bracelet's use.

There is a growing phenomenon of young single mothers in the cities. They have no government support, and tend to stay in the family home, but it is very hard for them to continue their education to a higher level.

In some rural areas there are curfews for children to leave the streets and return home, which may be signaled by a horn sounded at the fire station. This is usually around 9:00 p.m., and is aimed at protecting them. In any case it is not traditional for children to stay up late or attend evening parties.

PANAMANIAN HOUSES

Urban Panamanians strive to be independent, and despite rising prices many young people work hard to earn money for a place of their own, even if it is only one rented room. Basic accommodation starts from around U.S. $200 a month, but to rent a family house can be much more, especially in the better parts of the city. The average monthly wage is U.S. $350.

Panama has a wide variety of homes. The affluent spend a great deal on maintaining their residences, which are seen as a sign of wealth and status. In Panama City high-rise apartment blocks are most popular with moneyed couples, and detached, Spanish-style villa homes attract families. Other

demonstrations of wealth include manicured gardens, water features on the terrace, high security gates, and security guards for apartment blocks. Housing in rural areas consists mainly of basic concrete cinder block structures, often painted in bright colors. The blocks allow the buildings to "breathe," and keep them cool in rising humidity. It is also common to see thatched houses, on stilts in wet areas, accommodating rural Indians.

Casco Viejo (or San Felipe), Panama's second city, which has impressive colonial architecture, was recognized by UNESCO (along with Panamá Vieja) as a World Heritage Site. Casco Viejo was built in the seventeenth century and flourished for two hundred years before it fell into deep decline as twentieth-century Panama City developed. It became a very poor area, with many buildings that are now in need of extensive restoration. However, with government incentives, Casco Viejo has seen a remarkable transformation. Its glorious shuttered apartments are now characterized as colonial urban chic, and the property value in the area is rising. Colonial architecture also abounds in the historical city of Colón and the surrounding suburbs; however these areas are yet to enjoy renovation.

Another architecturally distinctive area is the Bocas del Toro archipelago. From the late nineteenth century the area was a thriving commercial and residential center for the region's banana trade, and the houses, especially on Isla Colón (although many have since been rebuilt) reflect Caribbean and New England architecture. The original houses are wooden, with wide verandas and ornate, painted gables.

DAILY LIFE

Civil and public employees begin their working day at 7:30 a.m. and usually finish at 3:30 p.m., with an hour for lunch. Those with children also rise early as school hours can also start from 7:30 a.m. Private business and office hours run from 9:00 or 10:00 a.m. until 4:00 or 5:00 p.m. Shops, hotels, restaurants, and security staff work on rota or shift systems. Throughout the day and night in Panama there is always someone at work, from international business dealing down to night security in banks, hotels, and offices. Even in some of Panama's most rural spots, local banks and shops usually have round-the-clock security guards. Further, it has been a recent government tactic to distribute working hours evenly in Panama City, to undo the gridlock of city traffic during morning and evening rush hours. This is perhaps why the city has such a lively twenty-four-hour atmosphere. Perhaps because of the long-standing U.S. influence, or the Panamanian love of a vibrant life, Panama City's lifestyle reflects that of any major Western city: people work very hard, and expect to play very hard.

This is not the case outside Panama City, where many Panamanians go to bed early and rise with the dawn to start work. This is particularly true of Indian people and fishermen, most of whom start work with the rising sun and sleep at sunset.

Sunday is the usual free day, though not for shiftworkers and business executives. Saturday is generally taken up with household chores; therefore Sunday is especially valued free time.

LEISURE TIME AND SHOPPING

Weekends are spent enthusiastically shopping, going out with friends for evening drinks, and dancing. Sunday for most Panamanians includes going to church and an afternoon out. In Panama

City, the Calzador de Amador (Amador Causeway), a paved walkway made from the rocks removed during the Canal's construction, is very popular for families and couples on a Sunday evening. Pedal cars and bikes can be rented. The Causeway joins four small islands, which are now home to modern restaurants and bars, boutiques, and the Smithsonian's Marine Exhibition Center.

There is a *joie de vivre* about Panamanians, who will work an exceptionally hard week without grumbling, but on a long weekend will pack their bags and race off to the country to relax. On normal weekends it is common to escape to the beach for at least a day, and, with the exception of the highlands, the majority of Panamanians are in fairly close proximity to pristine Pacific or Caribbean shores. Weekends that combine national holidays often create a four- or five-day break, so many city dwellers pack the car, or take the bus to the country to visit relatives. Others plan longer trips to Panama's Pacific or Caribbean islands, none of which are more than an hour away by plane.

There are several large supermarket chains throughout the country; some in larger cities are open twenty-four hours. However, Panamanians still love to shop locally, especially in country areas. Some of the freshest fruits and vegetables are found at local markets. In many neighborhoods, country people bring their own homegrown produce to town each week, and their entire stock will probably sell out within an hour or so. In small local stores everyday essentials are available in very small quantities, principally for poorer citizens.

EDUCATION

"*Kinder*," or nursery schools, are very popular for working mothers, and those who can afford it send their children from the age of three until they are six. Then, from six until twelve, primary school is compulsory for all Panamanian children. This includes Indian *comarcas*, where a Panamanian state-trained teacher attends schools in individual villages. Children attending school are divided into groups, the majority going to school from 7:30 a.m. to 1:30 p.m., and the rest during afternoon hours. This does not reflect individual ability, but simply spreads out numbers.

After primary school, education is not compulsory and a parent can choose whether a child should continue studying. On the whole, Panamanian children stay at school until they are at least eighteen; however, in poor rural areas education tends to finish earlier. Poorer families need their children to work at a younger age, and such children do not complete a full education.

This said, due to educational restructuring during the Torrijos years, Panamanian children now have increased access to schools and colleges and literacy standards have vastly improved. In the year 2000, adult literacy was rated at 92.5 percent. For those who can afford it, night schools and part-time colleges are becoming popular for adults who have missed out parts of their education, although they are usually out of reach for those in rural areas. Many young people now work to pay school fees to study English and vocational courses.

A recent reform now allows underage pregnant girls to continue their education in regular classes, whereas previously the only education open to them was at night school. Some parents think that being schooled alongside underage pregnant girls may negatively influence other children, and disapprove of this. In a country where abortion is illegal, this is an ongoing debate.

Learning English
English is compulsory in all government-run schools, although it is taught solely at elementary level. So while young people leaving school are familiar with English-language basics, those who

are not required to use it at work tend to forget much of it. Therefore, many Panamanians do not speak English. However, the buoyant tourist trade is changing this and individuals are returning to part-time education to learn English and so improve their employment prospects. Private schools are bilingual, and private students usually speak fluent English at graduation.

University

The University of Panama had, until recently, registered three-quarters of all Panamanian university students. There are now several public and private universities, including a number of North American establishments. State-financed universities are relatively affordable, and the numbers attending are rising. City dwellers are more likely to attend than those in the countryside.

AN ARMY LIFE?

There is no standing army in Panama today and young people are not therefore required by government to attend compulsory national service. Even during the days of Noriega's Panama Defense Forces (PDF) there was no general conscription. At that time, during the eighties, many young Panamanians wanting to excel in the armed forces actually left Panama to train with foreign military academies around Latin America, notably Peru and Colombia. This ensured they obtained a higher rank on their return to Panama. Currently Panamanians can choose to join the North American army, which has been popular during recent years, due to the travel opportunities and benefit schemes they offer.

HEALTH AND SERVICES

Health services in Panama are generally very good. Although services wavered during economic problems of the 1980s and '90s, since the opening of the Panama Canal, more investment in health care has seen Panama's health record improve vastly above the standards of some of its Central American neighbors. Severe tropical diseases were eradicated in most inhabited areas, and malaria was eradicated from Panama City. Health expenditure in 2002 was 8.9 percent of GDP, life expectancy is seventy-five years (2003), and infant mortality has dropped to 1.8 percent (2003) over the last fifty years.

Those in employment pay government taxes, from which health care and pensions are paid. Children are entitled to care under their parents' health coverage. For unemployed Panamanians, a *Centro de Salud* (health center) exists in nearly every town throughout the country, providing health care at low cost. The health centers provide regular checkups, vaccinations, and tests. They have a special community feel; the waiting room is often a lively hub where locals catch up on the gossip while waiting for their appointments. The centers offer help to foreigners, and there are usually pharmacies on-site.

One criticism of the health service in Panama, and in other Central American countries, is that some of the prescribed vaccinations are "out of date"—meaning that elsewhere some ingredients have been superseded as a result of new research. It is common that a vaccine now not used, or since updated, in Europe or North America will still be prescribed in Central American countries. Visitors, of course, have the choice of vaccination in their own countries; Panamanians can use only what is available.

Wealthy Panamanians opt for private health care, which, especially in Panama City, is excellent, and much cheaper than in hospitals in the U.S.A., or private hospitals in Britain. There are several large private hospitals in Panama City.

TV AND RADIO

Panamanians adore *telenovelas*. These melodramatic soap operas, many of which are made in Colombia and Mexico, are shown daily, and although at first glimpse there seems to be little distinguishing one from another, just ask any Panamanian, and you will soon have all the lowdown. Channel Telemetro is *novela central*. Slapstick humor is popular, along with situation comedies and shows in which ordinary people are portrayed as funny or foolish. Benny Hill and Mr. Bean are particular foreign favorites.

Radio stations are even more energetic. The most popular DJs speak at a high volume, shouting and laughing as they chat; the louder they are, the more appealing they are to listeners. Panamanians love music, and many rely on radios rather than CD players for dancing in the  home. Additionally, Panamanians prefer to get their news from the radio; most own or have easy access to a radio, and there are numerous programs available. In the past radio stations have been important for political broadcasting, and some governments have tried to control the information aired. During Noriega's time the government owned Radio Nacional, which broadcast throughout Panama; its offices were bombed amid Operation Just Cause in 1989. Today Panamanians enjoy political talk shows and debates on the radio.

chapter six

TIME OUT

Panamanians generally work very hard, and look forward to their leisure time. Weekends are especially important, as many have to rise early on weekdays. The most popular pastimes for those who can afford it in Panama City are weekend trips and visiting family and friends. City lovers adore the seaside, and short breaks to beach resorts and islands are traditional. Rural Panamanians enjoy days out, family cycle rides, and picnics.

During evenings and nights out, Panamanians love to dance. Dancing is something a visitor will notice everywhere. Apart from restaurant dining and dancing, there is dancing at most evening social events. Live pop music has become the choice for younger people, and most generations enjoy watching salsa and Latin bands. While most theatrical and classical music events are available only to those who can afford them, amateur dramatics are becoming more popular, with small groups springing up around the country.

FOOD AND DRINK

Panamanians love their food. While the country's cultural mix has created a capital city full of international flavors (French, Italian, Spanish, Greek, Chinese, and Japanese, and more), Panamanians themselves usually opt for traditional meals—a variety of staples cooked with long-established combinations of flavors. Most people, especially those living outside the city, normally eat at home. This is mainly because of the cost, but it does mean that home cooking is usually excellent.

Housewives typically have a pan of rice and a pot of beans always on the go, and simply add meat each day. Therefore their stews and beans build up immense flavor as fresh onions, garlic, and herbs have time to infuse. In rural areas, locals enjoy inviting people to eat with them, and you may find, even as a stranger, that you are invited to join people for lunch.

Typical Food

Panamanians eat a hearty breakfast, usually consisting of eggs and fried food, such as *hojaldres* (deep-fried dough), which can be served with *queso blanco* (white cheese); *carimañolas* (meat enveloped in yucca dough and deep-fried); *tortillas* (grated maize, deep-fried—not the floury Mexican type), or sausages.

Lunch and dinner are similar. *Sopa Sancocho* is Panama's national dish, and originates from the country's interior. The original recipe uses *gallina patio* (hand-raised chicken), yam, garlic, *culantro* (or cilantro, a thick-leaved variant of coriander), and seasoning. Today many extras are added, including yucca, potatoes, and ham. The soup is popular throughout the country and is labeled as a hangover cure and even an aphrodisiac.

Lunch is named simply *comida typica* (typical food), and always consists of rice, meat, and beans or lentils; the meat varies. *Arroz con pollo* (rice with chicken) is probably the most popular fare. It is served everywhere, and Panamanians never seem to tire of it. Alternatives include *bisteck* (beef), *res* (beef shoulder), *chuletta* (pork chops), and *pescado* (fish). These basics are in themselves not particularly tasty; it is the extras that make the dish. Meat is usually cooked in a sauce, or *salsa*, which is seasoned with onions, garlic, fresh herbs, and tomato paste. Fish is usually fried and served with garlic and lime juice. *Frijoles* (beans) can be black (*frijoles negros*) or red kidney beans (*frijoles rojos*, or *porrotos*), and are cooked with *culantro*, thyme, onions, garlic, and fresh tomato, which creates a rich, tasty, dark sauce. A plate will always arrive with a side dish, usually pasta in tomato *salsa*, or mashed potatoes, and a salad garnish; *ensalada de papas* (potato salad) is popular and made with potatoes, boiled eggs, and mayonnaise, and sometimes prawns. Slices of fried plantain (a type of large, starchy banana) complete the dish.

Panama has yet to discover the notion of a plate consisting of one example of each food group. Notions such as "food combining" are unheard of, and Panamanian people are quite happy to have three starches—rice, potato, and pasta—on the same plate. For a nation that knows all too well the harsh reality of poverty, food is eaten with gratitude.

Seafood

Given the location of this tiny isthmus between two great oceans, seafood is, not surprisingly, very popular. There are vast fish markets in Panama City, but in rural areas, local Indians supply some of the freshest fresh seafood in the country. This remains an integral part of their economy and produce is caught by traditional methods. *Ceviche* is the most popular fish dish in Panama. It is made with *corvina* (white fish), onion, *culantro*, seasoning, and a touch of *picante* (hot *salsa*) marinated in fresh lime, which "cooks" the fish and onion. Variations include *camarones* (shrimp) and *pulpo* (octopus). It is served with plain crackers.

Buen Provecho

It's good manners to wish diners "*Buen provecho*" (*Bon appétit*) as an everyday courtesy. You will find that even strangers murmur this to you as they pass your table. Acknowledge this with a simple "*Gracias,*" as you carry on with your meal. People will appreciate your wishing them the same as you pass their tables.

Caribbean Specialties

Culinary flavors change on Panama's Atlantic shores, where Caribbean traditions blend with Spanish and Indian. Caribbean cooking is a great social event, and women often spend the

afternoon together preparing rice and vegetables on the veranda while exchanging local gossip. The most famous dish is coconut rice and beans, which are cooked separately in fresh coconut milk and served mixed together. Coconut rice can also be served with *gungo* (pigeon peas), known locally as *guandú*, which are green from the can, but if cooked fresh from the bush, turn the rice a striking shade of purple.

Coconuts are available straight from the tree. The flesh is tirelessly grated by hand, and squeezed to create milk and cream (milk mixed with sugar), which are used for rice, curries, breads, sweets, and *piña colada* (rum, pineapple, milk, and coconut cream). Coconut oil, made by heating and cooling the milk and collecting the separating fat, is used for cooking, frying, and on the hair (it turns it red in the sun) and skin. Other coconut favorites are Johnny cakes (bread made with coconut milk) and *cocada* (grated coconut mixed with melted sugar) eaten as a sweet or served with cinnamon bread.

Patacones, perhaps the most popular Caribbean snack, are lightly fried slices of green plantain, squashed and then deep-fried until crisp. They are usually eaten dipped in *picante*.

Street Favorites

Street snacks are cheap and often filling, and there's a wide range of tastes to experience. A favorite end of evening bite, found throughout the country, are *salchicha* barbecues—hotdogs and beef kebabs on a stick, usually served with a flour tortilla.

Empanadas and *tamales* are usually handmade, and are available everywhere. *Empanadas* are fried dough turnovers with chicken or beef, and occasionally cheese, inside. *Tamales* are made from corn, usually with chicken, wrapped and steamed

in *bijao* or plantain leaves. Panamanian *tamales* are thought to differ from those in neighboring countries in their added flavors of olives, capers, and herbs.

In some areas of Chiriquí and the central highlands *mielmesabe*, a sweetmeat made of sugarcane and honey, is sold with a piece of *queso blanco* (crumbly white cheese) wrapped in a banana leaf. It is traditional to eat the two together, as the flavors enhance each other. In cities, homemade *bollo* (creamed cooked maize) is sold wrapped in corn leaves, and has a surprisingly sweet flavor.

Another favorite with adults and children alike is *raspado*—ice shavings covered with sweet syrup and topped with evaporated milk and honey.

Finally, fruit is abundant and fresh. Everyday fruits don't need to be imported; they are also extremely cheap. Jams, juices, and ices are made with seasonal fruits. Green mango slices are sold in sandwich bags with a pinch of salt, vinegar, and *picante* for twenty-five cents. Peeled oranges are sold for five cents. Mangoes, oranges, papayas, melon, and banana are popular in fruit salads.

Desserts

Postres, or desserts, are traditional endings to meals, and for Panamanians the sweeter the better. Some of the most popular are *pastel tres leches* (a sponge cake soaked in milk, cream and evaporated milk), *puddin* (a heavy Caribbean cake made with yucca or banana), and sweet *empanadas* usually filled with *piña* (pineapple).

The Argentinean *dulce de leche* is also popular, both spread on sweet breads and sold in packets with coconut sweets.

Drinks

Panama grows excellent coffee in the central highlands. While the export business is still young and relatively small, there are several very reputable coffee companies in the country. Additionally for coffee lovers, several small family companies produce beans from private estates and most companies are happy to show visitors their coffee-making techniques, which include sun-drying the beans.

That said, Panamanians traditionally boil their coffee grounds, which makes a strong-tasting, nutty-flavored coffee. Also, coffee may be drunk with evaporated milk, especially outside the city, as fresh milk doesn't last long in the tropics.

Pipas (green, unripe coconuts) are available straight from the tree throughout Panama. Panamanians will climb up towering palm trees to pull coconuts down, or push them off the branches with long sticks. There are short palm trees, should you want to try climbing yourself (choose one over a sandy beach in case of a fall!), and a penknife will take the top off the coconut. *Pipa* water is a great way to avoid dehydration on a hot day out and *pipas* are perfect for long days on the beach or when walking in the hot city, where they are sold refrigerated in food stores, and on the streets.

The Panamanian *chicherme* is a traditional drink made by boiling dry, cracked corn, and adding milk and cinnamon. There is an alcoholic version of this; brewed mainly in the interior, it is hard to find, and is not sold in stores.

Chichas are the much more wholesome equivalent of fruit squash, made from fresh fruit, water, and sugar. Some include grains, *avena* (oats) and *arroz* (rice) and milk. They are sold in cafeterias throughout the country, and even adult Panamanians usually choose a *chicha* to accompany their meal, rather than an alcoholic drink, which is preferred after eating (except at dinner parties). Also regularly drunk are the cheap and excellent *batidos*—fruit juices freshly blended with milk or ice.

Beer is the most popular alcoholic drink in Panama, from a male perspective at least; women tend to drink cocktails and wine. Panamanian beers are very cheap, served exceptionally cold, and seen as the ultimate refreshment on a hot, humid day. The main brews are Balboa, Atlas, Panama, and Soberana, which are all similar in alcohol content and fairly mild.

Wine is also enjoyed, and the Chilean Concha y Toro is the most widely drunk. Panamanians love their drinks cold, and visitors will notice that even red wine is often served from the fridge.

Panama's national liquor, Seco Herrerano, is an extremely strong spirit distilled from sugarcane. It is locally known as *siete letras*, from the seven letters of Herrera, the province from which it originates. Panamanians love it, and at *fiesta* time coolers full of bottles of Seco appear in the street. It is traditionally drunk with milk, but is now more popular with Coca-Cola, ice, and a slice of lime, much like a "Cuba libre."

EATING OUT

Basic cafés known as *fondas* serve traditional food very cheaply. There is usually a set lunch or dinner each day, with a choice of meats. These plates are labeled, simply, *comida* (food). *Fondas* tend to close early in the evening, as most locals eat before 8:00 p.m. However, in the city the big restaurants are open late, some for the full twenty-four hours.

Many Panamanians work a six-day week, so free days are valuable to them, and families and couples often have a long, relaxed Sunday lunch in a restaurant. Fast-food outlets are becoming increasingly popular, however, especially with young people and families, mainly because their prices are so low. Now, in the cities, McDonald's, KFC, and Burger King rival the traditional *fondas*.

TIPPING

In restaurants a 10 percent service charge is usually already added to the bill. You do not need to tip on top of this. However, wealthy Panamanians tip a little more if they are pleased with the service; you will make a waiter's day if you do the same, not just because of the boost to his wages but, with typical Panamanian pride, he will feel he has done his job well. If you wish to tip a particular individual, give it to him or her personally; otherwise leave it on the table or with the bill.

Tipping in hotels is only expected in high-level establishments, but you may wish to ensure the best service in a mid-level hotel by tipping porters and cleaners.

Taxi drivers don't expect tips either, but they are very pleased to get one.

NIGHTLIFE AND MUSIC

Nightlife thrives in the city where there are numerous bars and clubs, most of which do not get busy until late. Panamanians like to relax and eat during the earlier part of the evening, so the nightlife starts around 10:00 or 11:00 p.m. Most bars are open until at least 2:00 a.m., and clubs much later. The clubs in Panama City are sophisticated, and look like clubs in any other modern city. Several establishments play rock music, and electronic dance music is also popular. However, Panamanians tend to dress more smartly than clubbers in other countries. Women wear the traditional little black dress and men wear shirts, sometimes ties. It is unlikely that you will be turned away from regular nightclubs for wearing jeans and sneakers, but you are recommended to dress up rather than down.

Many clubs in Panama City run a weekly Ladies' Night, where women may get in free, and in some cases even drink free until midnight. Not surprisingly, these nights can often be the most popular of the week, for both men and women.

Salsa and merengue are widely listened to, and Panama has its own range of homebred stars. Perhaps the most famous is the Latin singer, salsa, and movie star Rubén Blades, who is known not just in Panama, but throughout the Latin music scene. However, Panamanians particularly admire him for his largely left-wing political commitment to the country, and in 1994 he ran (unsuccessfully) for Panamanian president. He is now tourist minister in Panama. Panamanian musical duo Sammy and Sandra Sandoval are also well loved, and play romantic, Latin-style salsa.

Jazz is becoming increasingly popular. An annual festival has been held in Panama City since 2003, organized by Panamanian contemporary jazz pianist and composer Danilo Pérez, and featuring Panamanian jazz musicians. Other popular music among young people in Panama includes reggae and reggaeton (a unique style of Spanish rap and reggae), western rock and pop music and within the city, *electronica* (modern dance music) and breakbeats. Other Panamanian musicians include Edgardo "El General" Franco, who helped put rap on the Latin American music scene, and Los Rabanes, a popular rock band.

Nightlife in rural areas is very different from that in the city. Some local bars cater mainly to men, and can be intimidating for women. Also, during weekends and vacations, crowds who have indulged in too much alcohol congregate in local bars and *cantinas*, and occasionally an evening will end with a fight and flying bottles. Visitors should never get involved, and locals will usually have the ruckus sorted out in a matter of minutes.

DANCING

The Panamanians' love of *fiesta* goes hand-in-hand with their urge to dance. Indians in Panama have performed ceremonial dances for centuries, and this is still an integral part of their culture. The Spanish invasion introduced a further set of moves to the country, and Panamanians today will tell you that dancing is in their blood. Housewives dance at home during the day to the radio, and with their husbands after dinner. At evenings out there is always a dance floor, and even after a dinner party the table will be moved aside to make room for salsa. Panamanians are taught to dance from an early age, and children as young as six know the difference between dance moves. In bars and clubs throughout the country people from eighteen to eighty will spend their evenings dancing. To see Panamanians dance is impressive, as movements are fluid and inspired. Additionally, even in a country where it is generally inappropriate for a man to approach another's girlfriend, an invitation to join one in a dance is viewed as entirely normal. Salsa and merengue are the most popular styles, along with *bachata* and *cumbia* music rhythms.

SPORTS

Many Panamanians are sporty, and enjoy keeping fit. In Panama City you'll see joggers, cyclists, and the occasional rollerblader along the Amador Causeway and Avenida Balboa (the main road that runs alongside the Pacific Ocean). In rural areas you can always find a game of football going on. However, chiefly due to economics and work hours, most Panamanians prefer to be spectators rather than players.

American sports are popular, not surprisingly, and baseball is the favorite. Many professional Panamanian players have joined major league baseball in North America, and Panama's most famous player was Rod Carew, although Panama itself has not had a professional team since the 1970s. A new Panamanian league has recently been formed that includes some major players, and the country has high hopes for their professional future.

Baseball aside, boxing is arguably Panama's most loved sport, and this not only attracts viewers, but produces world champions, one after the other. Panama has now reared twenty-three world champions and Panamanians, proud of their achievements, fondly describe their land as a "little country with world boxing power." The love of the game cuts across class, and it is normal to find boxing matches shown on big screens in some of the most sophisticated bars in the city. Additionally, Panamanian citizens judge their national boxers harshly, knowing virtually everything about the art of boxing themselves.

Roberto Duran, nicknamed "Manos de Piedra" ("Hands of Stone"), is perhaps Panama's most famous boxer, fighting in five decades and winning titles in four different weight classes. He retired in 2002, at the age of fifty-two. Excitement now surrounds Roberto Vásquez, nicknamed "La Araña" ("The Spider") who became Super Featherweight Champion in 2005 and the first Latin American to have held three titles at the same time. Celestino "Pelenchin" Caballero also won the world title lightweight champion of the World Boxing Association in 2005, and it seems there may be many more rising boxing stars in the wings. Big fights are now usually held at the Figali Convention Center in Panama City.

Football (soccer) is not revered in Panama quite as it is in other Latin countries, but it is a popular local sport and played most Sundays throughout the country, from impromptu five-a-sides to competing provincial teams. The national football team (controlled by the Federación Panameña de Fútbol) has never qualified for the World Cup, although it made the final regional qualifying round for the 2006 World Cup.

Some of the world's most renowned surfing waves are found in the country, including Santa Catalina on the Pacific and the notorious Silver Back that swells in the Bocas del Toro Archipelago. Both visitors and Panamanians participate. Other common sports include rowing (boat races are held annually in Taboga and the Panama Canal) and fishing.

SHOPPING OPPORTUNITIES

City shopping is very different from shopping in rural areas, where things are generally bought only as and when needed. In Panama's three main cities, however, shopping and window-shopping are common and in Panama City the shopping opportunities are extensive. The wealthy cruise from designer shop to designer shop by car—walking is not popular—in the expensive Marbella and central areas of the city. A number of vast malls are a recent addition to Panama City, most of which feature top designer labels. For those unable to afford the real thing, the numerous cavernous stores lining Avenida Central from Via España to Calidonia are brimming with bargains. These stores also sell designer labels—either last year's leftovers, or copies—at bargain-basement prices. Shop hours are 9:00 a.m. to 8:00 p.m., Monday to Saturday. Most large malls are also open on Sundays.

For foreigners, the shopping possibilities are even greater. The Colón Free Zone is enormous, and while the Free Zone is a wholesale market, visitors can sometimes buy duty-free products to be sent to the airport and collected once through immigration. There are several other major duty-free shops in Panama, including the Panama Canal Village in Colón, and a large store on Flemenco Island on the Amador Causeway.

Traditional Panamanian arts, crafts, and souvenirs are sold throughout the country. Kuna, Embera, and Ngöbe Indians sell their wares in large market stalls, and in small individual stalls in tourist spots. All their wares are handmade, and every item is unique. The money goes straight to the families who made them, and the trade helps the well-being of the community as a whole. In Panama City

there are craft markets in tourist spots such as Miraflores Locks and Panamá Vieja. A great market in the heart of the city is Mercado Artesanal Cinco de Mayo, located behind the old anthropological museum on Plaza Cinco de Mayo.

PANAMA HATS

A Panama hat sounds like the ideal souvenir; however, the original product is, and always has been, made in Ecuador. The cream straw hat was termed a "Panama" because of its popularity among the workers who needed protection from the sun during the construction of the Panama Canal. The hats are widely available in Panama. An authentic one can be folded without creasing.

Panamanians themselves have their own style of hat, also woven and not so flexible, but uniquely Panamanian. These hats are predominantly made in the rural interior and are woven with different styles of bands and patterns denoting the originating area.

Librería Cultural Panameña, S.A., located on Avenida España in the Perejil area, is a small bookshop with a wonderful selection of Panamanian literature and history (mostly in

Spanish). Some large department stores in Panama City also stock Indian arts, books, and illustrated history.

CULTURAL ACTIVITIES

As more opportunities arise for young people to study to a higher level, Panamanian students are developing a new interest in their own culture. Many want to travel to study the art and history of other countries, but most want to return to Panama to use their knowledge to promote awareness of Panama's own cultural history.

The number of museums is growing. A new visitor center has been built at Panamá Vieja, where human and historical remains still lie covered. The Panama Canal Museum, located in Casco Viejo, is extensive and informative. Additionally, the Museo Antropológico Dr. Reina Torres de Araúz, which is currently being relocated to Currundú, has a stunning collection of *huacas*—gold and pottery excavated from ancient tombs. The new Biodiversity Museum at the entrance to the Amador Causeway will be inaugurated in 2006. Designed by Frank O. Gehry, it seeks to represent Panama's unique and complex natural diversity. Panama's offshoot of the Smithsonian Institution in Washington has contributed to its development.

GAMBLING

Sellers for the Panamanian lottery, La Loteria Nacional de Beneficencia, seem to follow you wherever you go, popping into restaurants, buses, and local shops, and sitting in strategic positions in parks and on street corners. Played twice a week, on Wednesdays and Sundays, the lottery is government-owned, with profits going to hospitals and local charities. Panamanians love it, and regularly try their luck.

Casinos tower over the city streets, in Panama City in particular. There are reportedly around four hundred gambling establishments—so many that the government has recently stopped granting new licenses. Some of the casinos are huge, ranging from high buildings covered in lights to less conspicuous gambling halls. They are usually open twenty-four hours. Although Panamanians love to gamble, this is more likely to be in local bingo sessions and weekly lottery draws than at blackjack and poker.

Cockfighting, sadly, is common in the countryside; however its popularity has declined.

THE SEAMIER SIDE

Panama has been associated with drugs and arms smuggling for a long while, a reputation reinforced in novels and movies. The glittering high-rises of Panama City's Punta Paitilla, a peninsula in the Pacific, have been dubbed "Cocaine Towers" in fiction. Despite this, tourists and visitors will probably never witness such goings-on. In general street crime in Panama is at an all-time low, and new tourism initiatives have driven a rise in tourist police in shadier parts of the city. As with all major cities, there are several dangerous "downtown" areas, which should be avoided, especially at night.

Prostitution is legal and widespread, predominantly in the city but also in some provincial areas. Brothels are common, although not always visible; many go unnoticed unless someone is specifically looking for one. In many cases it is not a taboo question to ask about prostitutes. However, visitors should bear in mind that, as is typical throughout the world, girls are often working out of desperation. Many have come from Colombia and the Dominican Republic. There are numerous lap-dancing bars and strip clubs, and most hotels do not raise an eyebrow if a room is rented by the hour.

TRAVELING

ENTRY REQUIREMENTS AND VISAS

As a tourist, you can stay in Panama for ninety days. For more time in the country, you must either apply for an extension at a regional National Immigration Bureau or leave the country and stay away for seventy-two hours before reentering. You will need proof of a return ticket (or a ticket out of the country) and economic solvency. After a further ninety days, if you wish to extend your stay again, you will need to leave the country for seventy-two hours.

Citizens from most Western European countries need only a valid passport to enter Panama. Citizens from the United States, Canada, Australia, and some Asian and Caribbean countries also need a tourist card. These are obtainable from airlines and travel agencies. Citizens from parts of Africa, the Philippines, Thailand, Peru, and the Dominican Republic need a stamped visa.

GETTING ABOUT

Panamanians love vacations, and all leisure time is precious. Public holidays are usually arranged around a weekend, so great is the importance of a break. Weekends throughout the dry season are often spent at the beach, and longer vacations are planned months in advance. City families commonly return to their ancestral homes in the country when they can, so the cities can be oddly quiet at vacation times.

Traveling around Panama by bus or plane is easy and enjoyable, partly because the scenery can change drastically within relatively short distances. For example, while driving from David on the Pacific to Bocas del Toro on the Caribbean, the road leaves the hot, dusty city, enters rural farmland, passes through rolling volcanic hills and valleys, and emerges into lush, humid, tropical forest.

Flying

Domestic flights are frequent and reliable and make traveling exceptionally efficient. You can fly to almost any destination in the country in less than an hour. Panamanian businesspeople prefer to fly, so during weekdays, flights between the country's three main cities of Panama, Colón, and David are usually packed. Unlike their English and American counterparts, who see commuting as a dreary trudge from A to B, Panamanian commuters who fly are stress-free travelers who enjoy the company or the scenery, or are simply catching up with the daily newspaper. The flight is seen as a chance to relax before the day's work, so you may well find yourself chatting to a commuter on your flight.

The planes are small, turbo-propelled, and seat between thirty-six and forty-six passengers, which can be unnerving for those more accustomed to jumbos. However, flights are short and the views can be spectacular, so keep your camera on hand.

On checking in, you will be for asked your weight (you can jump on the baggage scales if you are not sure). Don't be shy—no Panamanian bats an eyelid about this. There are usually limits on baggage weight and you will be charged for excess. If you are carrying heavy bags or boxes, you can ship them as cargo on the same flight.

Panama's main domestic service is Aeroperlas (a subsidiary of Taca International Airlines), which flies to twenty-six destinations in the country. There are several other smaller companies, including Air Panama and Ansa. Occasional deals are offered for students.

Book well in advance during holidays. Although extra flights usually operate during Carnaval, they may be fully booked months ahead.

Buses

A far cry from the proverbial Central American Chicken Bus, Panama's bus system is known as one of the best transportation services in Central America. An excellent range of modern coaches and minibuses operates throughout the country. The buses are slightly more expensive than those in other Central American countries, but the service is much better. Despite the Panamanian tendency to be late, buses tend to be very reliable and can get booked up, so, again, it is advisable to book in advance.

It is not just visitors who can't cope with tropical heat and humidity—Panamanians don't like it either, so most long-distance services are fitted with air-conditioning. It's important to note that air-conditioned buses get very cold on long rides. Panamanians come extremely well prepared for long-distance bus travel, usually with pillows and blankets. Long-distance coaches usually have toilets, and make stops at roadside cafés. El Expreso (fast) buses run on routes between major cities, often show movies (usually in Spanish), and provide comfier seats. All buses are nonsmoking.

Don't expect much conversation with locals on long journeys, as most are asleep by the time they leave the bus station. However, on local, rural routes, while conversation is not expected,

Panamanians will say "*Buenas*" (literally, "Good," short for "Good day" or "Good afternoon") to the whole bus on entering. Everyone on the bus replies "*Buenas*" in unison, and nothing more is said. Panamanian strangers are a communal people, but have a great respect for privacy.

A Word of Warning

The major bus terminal in Panama City is well policed, but Colón bus terminal has a bad reputation. Use caution in all bus terminals, especially in cities, as they are a favorite (and sometimes most lucrative) haunt of pickpockets. Do as Panamanians do themselves—keep watch, and have at least one hand on your belongings at all times, even if you are approached by someone who appears very friendly. Bear in mind that they may be working with someone else who plans to swipe your bag as you chat.

URBAN TRANSPORTATION

Buses

Unlike the sturdy dependability of the national buses, buses in Panama City are a law unto themselves. Nicknamed "*Diablos Rojos*" (Red Devils), these overused ex-U.S. school buses are souped-up beasts of the metropolis. Their owners go to great lengths to decorate them, and you will

find them adorned with hand-painted murals
spreading from nose to tail. Pictures show Jesus
and the Virgin Mary, cartoon characters, owners'
girlfriends and mothers, various Panamanian
scenes and slogans, and more besides. Inside they
can be just as colorful, the drivers' cab festooned

with flashing lights,
dangly toys, and
crushed velvet. Loud
music on the buses is
in theory now
outlawed, but there
seems to be some
dispute as to the exact definition of "loud," so be
prepared for some rowdy salsa to carry you to
your destination.

Finally, be aware that these drivers have a
reputation for racing each other. It is not
uncommon to find your bus in a race against
another multicolored *Diablo*. Local passengers do
not seem to pay much attention to this revving
and spitting between buses, so stay relaxed. A ride
on *El Diablo Rojo* now costs twenty-five cents in
central zones, usually payable as you leave the bus.

Taxis
It is common for Panamanians in cities to take
taxis everywhere, as walking is not popular. Taxis
operate throughout the city, on a zone system,

starting at U.S. $1.25 in the central zone, with
twenty-five cents added for each extra person.
Authorized taxis are recognizable by a white block
with black numbers on the side of the car. Don't
be surprised if your taxi looks as though it has
failed a few road tests. Many taxis on the road are
in need of repair, but if one looks too daunting,
politely turn it down and wait for another. Wear
the seat belt—drivers can be speedy.

Most taxi drivers are very friendly and will ask
where you are from and how you like Panama.
They are invariably proud of their country, and if
you are able to speak some Spanish they will
happily point out interesting sights. A driver who
may not know exactly how to reach your
destination will cheerfully drive off regardless,
stopping to ask for directions and taking you
round in circles, but he is trying to be helpful, so
contain your frustration. Drivers don't expect tips
(but it will make their day to get one).

Trains
There are just two railroads in Panama. The
historic Panama–Colón railway was built in 1855.
It took five years to complete, cost eight million
U.S. dollars, and provided a safer route for North
Americans heading to the San Francisco gold
rush. It continued to function after the Panama
Canal was opened, but was abandoned in 1979.

Some ten years later, Panama finally privatized the railroad, and over a million U.S. dollars were put into its restoration. Today, a historic train (bought from Florida) operates a service, predominantly for tourists, along the side of the Canal, and through some parts of it, between Panama City and Colón.

The country's second railroad carries the banana train that runs through the northern end of the Bocas del Toro province, by the border with Costa Rica. The train is integral to one of Panama's biggest exports: more than four million bananas are exported from Panama per day. Interested travelers sometimes seek permission to hop aboard, however this is not advisable—it does not serve as a passenger train, and it goes incredibly slowly!

DRIVING

The reliably paved Pan-American Highway (or Interamericana) splits the country lengthways in two, and offers easy access to major destinations. Off the highway most roads around and between key locations are paved and well maintained, but as you go further into the country, paved roads become badly paved roads, and then dirt roads, only passable with a four-wheel drive vehicle, so check maps first.

Holes in the road appear quite frequently, due to the climate, and care should be taken, especially off the main highway where repairs can take time. Additionally, around the central highland region in the provinces of Chiriquí and Bocas del Toro roads can be subject to minor landfalls; it is therefore wise not to travel at night.

The Pan-American Highway ends at Yaviza in the Darién. Over recent years there have been various plans to lengthen the road through the Colombian border to meet its South American counterpart, but so far the dense Darién jungle has proved impenetrable. Additionally there are very many environmental concerns over these plans.

Many Panamanians love cars and driving, and those who can afford it have four-wheel drive vehicles, which are often essential in the countryside. Panamanians are known for their hospitality, and one common example given is their willingness to help other drivers whose cars have broken down.

Rental cars and four-wheel-drive vehicles are available throughout the country, with main offices in Panama City. Be sure to check the insurance details with your rental car—some smaller companies may not cover everything.

Note that the speed limit on main highways is 62 miles (100 km) per hour, and also that police may pull you over if you are not wearing a seat belt, or if they suspect you have been drinking alcohol.

City Driving

Driving in Panama City can be eventful, and is best left to experienced drivers. City speed limits are 37 miles (60 km) per hour, but it seems that whenever possible, and especially at night, the limit is ignored. Local city drivers can be speedy, reckless, and pushy, and will beep their horn simply for having to slow down. They may change lanes with little warning, and rarely make way for other cars. While it is recommended to give other drivers a wide berth, if you don't show some confidence you may be stuck for a long while at intersections.

"*Tranque*" is the word that Panamanians use for slow-moving traffic. Rush hours tend to build up quickly, and can be unbearable in the steaming city heat. The government is reviewing work hours and other ways in which excessive traffic can be reduced in the city. Having said this, city dwellers enjoy cruising around in their cars, and between the rush hours the roads are still busy, with many drivers simply out for a drive. Not many people walk in Panama—even the poor would rather get on a bus. Taxis are popular, but anyone who can afford it will drive a car.

Driving Tips

Keep belted up. Panamanians themselves are still reluctant to use seat belts and will not expect visitors to do so either. However, the police are cracking down on this, and, especially in the city, it is better to be safe.

During the years of political turmoil and a struggling economy, wages were low. Police throughout Latin America, often trying to support large families, commonly stopped and fined drivers for no reason—an extra twenty dollars could mean next week's food. This is now a very rare occurrence, and it is most unlikely to happen to you. However, just in case it does, it is much easier to pay a fine (which would normally be minimal) and be on your way; fighting it risks a long evening at the police station.

Keep your passport handy. It is illegal not to carry it, or a copy of it, or at the very least some form of photo ID in all situations, not just when traveling. While driving you may come across police checkpoints, usually in the vicinity of border patrols. You may also be asked to open your trunk by officers checking for drugs and arms trafficking.

WHERE TO STAY

Panamanians use hotels frequently, for business and pleasure. Therefore good accommodation is available at reasonable prices. In Panama City, you can find a clean hotel room with air-conditioning, a hot shower en suite, and cable TV for around U.S. $25 (you pay for the room, not per person). For higher budgets there is a range of luxurious traditional and chain hotels with pools, spas, and even butler service.

For this reason, the budget traveler will not need to venture into the seedy parts of town to find a cheap room. Even the local backpacker's hostel is situated in the best area of town. The safest areas to look for hotels are Punta Paitilla, El Cangrejo, Marbella, and Bella Vista, and you will find the most reputable establishments here.

Outside the city, prices rise a little, but are still relatively cheap compared with other tourist destinations. Options range from large resorts to nature-inspired beach or jungle cabins, or *cabiñas*, family-run bed and breakfast establishments, hostels (*hospedajes*), and camping sites. Hotels charge a 10 percent tax.

HEALTH

Most towns have a clinic (*Centro de Salud*, see Chapter 5) or small hospital, and are able to deal with minor problems. Panamanians are very practical, it is worth noting. Some of the things you might find alarming, such as a scorpion bite, can be quite common, and they will give sensible advice and not fuss unnecessarily. The costs of minor treatments, such as stitches and antibiotics, are very low.

Remote areas may have medical facilities only available on a weekly basis, or none at all. Travelers should therefore carry first-aid supplies, especially if planning a trip off the beaten path. Essential items are insect repellent, antihistamine, alcohol, or alcohol wipes or patches, for cleaning wounds, antiseptic cream, plasters, bandages, and diarrhea and rehydration remedies. Hikers and jungle trekkers should add water purifying tablets and hypodermic needles. Good kits can be bought from backpacking and travel shops. Sun block is crucial. You should always carry some with you as the weather, especially in Caribbean regions, is temperamental—an overcast morning can quickly become a scorching afternoon.

Malaria has been eradicated in Panama City, and is rare in most tourist areas west of Panama City, although you may be advised to take basic malaria prevention if you plan to visit the provinces of Bocas del Toro and Veraguas. However, those venturing into the Darién will need suitable malaria prevention.

Dengue fever also occurs in Panama, although is relatively rare for travelers to be affected. It is thought to be carried by a day-biting mosquito, and produces flulike symptoms. It is called "*rompa huesa*" (break-bone fever) by some locals. These strains are not fatal, although there is a further, rare strain of the virus that can be.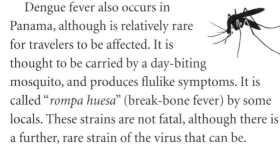

In some areas, Panamanians will chuckle to themselves if tourists ask about malaria or dengue fever. This will imply that you are in no danger where you are staying. The Panamanians are not unrealistic, and many will explain that it is only in remote villages and jungle areas that one needs to worry about such infections. Locals take extra precautions these days to keep malaria and dengue at bay by the proper management of stagnant water (mosquito breeding ground).

Avoid bites by covering up at dusk and late afternoons when the mosquitoes appear. Keep repellent on and sleep under a mosquito net if you are staying in rural areas.

NATURAL HAZARDS

Panamanians in rural areas are accustomed to jellyfish, scorpions, snakes, and spiders, and not only these, but also crocodiles, alligators, and the occasional angry dog. Locals have ways to avoid and deal with these creatures, and the best advice is to watch them. For example, a rural Panamanian will instinctively walk with a heavy tread in jungle, grassy, and some coastal areas to keep snakes away. There is a Panamanian saying that snakes will not bite pregnant women, however, it is still best to stamp loudly! Checking under logs for scorpions when sitting in rural areas is routine, as is choosing the right time to travel by river to avoid crocodiles.

It's likely that the most bothersome creatures you will come across are "fire ants," which drive the locals crazy. Once bitten you will never again take your flip-flops off on the grass. These tiny ants cause a burning sting that, while harmless, can itch for days. Applying vinegar can help.

SAFETY
As in any foreign country, it is good on arrival to ask locals which are the safe and unsafe parts of the region you are staying in. Panamanians are particularly aware of foreigners' vulnerability, and if you wander into unsafe areas you may find that concerned locals will attempt to warn you of the dangers. Having said this, crime levels in Panama are lower than they have ever been.

The jungles of the Darién continue to pose a safety problem, and visitors should research routes and take advice if they are intending to travel in the area. Drug traffickers and Colombian militant guerrillas occupy areas of the Darién Gap, and a number of tourists have been kidnapped while attempting to cross from Panama to Colombia. However, although not advisable, it is possible to cross the border by boat from the Caribbean side.

PLACES TO VISIT
Panama City

Panama City these days is most often labeled "cosmopolitan," and on visiting the city you will understand why. Undisputedly a thoroughly U.S.-influenced city, it is its Panamanian aspects that make it so vibrant, attractive, and remarkable. The U.S. influence makes it easy and available. Panama City's glittering center and vast shopping malls are interspersed with energetic street life, hand-painted billboards, and huge trees festooned with creepers that dangle in your path, while the roots push up the pavement beneath your feet.

Additionally, the city is interwoven with colonial and early twentieth-century history. The ruins of Panamá Vieja lie to the east of the city and areas among the ruins are still being excavated. The crumbling Casco Viejo (see page 88) is studded with colonial churches, and architectural relics not touched since the turn of the last century. The picturesque and pristinely kept Calzada Amador provides a relaxing city escape along with fantastic views of the Bridge of the Americas and the city skyline.

Islands and National Parks

There are around 1,500 islands of varying sizes surrounding Panama. The most visited islands are the Bocas del Toro archipelago, Las Perlas, and San Blas; the former two have been used as locations for the television series *Survivor*.

Island life on both the Pacific and the Caribbean is laid-back and relaxed, though culturally they differ greatly. New resorts on the still relatively uninhabited Las Perlas islands now attract golfing, fishing, and sailing tourism; while in Bocas del Toro you will find a chiefly Caribbean ambience with exotic flavors and music.

San Blas is home to the self-governing Kuna people (see pages 15-17), who are dedicated to the conservation of their 365 islands and parts of the surrounding mainland. This has become a precious gift for Panama; as resorts, roads, and businesses are constructed on other islands in the country, the Kuna hope the islands of San Blas will remain as they have always been: an all-natural habitat. With luck and governmental support their wish will be upheld.

Panama harbors an incredible array of wildlife—200 mammal species, of which 125 are native, approximately 950 bird species, which is more than North America and Europe combined, and around 10,000 plant species. It is not surprising that the country attracts so many naturalists, especially during October, when birds are migrating. Panama's main national parks are La Amistad (Chiriquí), Barro Colorado Island (Gatun Lake, Panama Canal), Bastimentos National Marine Park (Bocas del Toro), Soberania and Metropolitan (Panama City), Volcan Baru, Isla de Coiba, and the Darién.

chapter eight

BUSINESS BRIEFING

From gold trading in colonial times to today's Canal commerce, business has always been an important feature of life in Panama. Owing to the U.S.A.'s major contribution to Panama's trading history, business practice in Panama City is thoroughly American, with a sophisticated business and professional life that largely follows modern Western norms. Colón, Panama's second-largest city, is not as modern or as luxurious, but a number of commercial areas— particularly the Colón Free Zone—have been developed out of the surrounding urban poverty. Panama City and Colón, located at each end of the Canal, are key locations for trade and business in the country.

The Panamanian business style, while fast-moving and efficient, retains the Latin "relaxed" approach. However, you should understand, if your agreements and documents take a while to be completed, that this will usually be because of bureaucracy and red tape rather than laxity on the part of your corporate contacts.

Traditionally, businesses in Panama are family-owned, and although most leading companies are professionally managed, it is common to find family members throughout upper management levels. Business recommendations, too, may arise from family connections, so don't be surprised to find a tightly knit community behind more than one deal you negotiate. Nepotism has been present in Panamanian society since the rise of the oligarchy at the turn of the twentieth century. However, times are changing, and the country has seen the growth of multinational corporations in the banking and shipping sectors over the last few decades, and more recently in fields such as communications and brewing. Even so, many firms in Panama are still run as personal fiefdoms.

THE BUSINESS CULTURE

Because business in Panama is a happy mix of modern American style and Latin customs, the whole procedure should be slightly less stressful than one might expect. One of the most crucial points to remember is the importance placed on long-standing work relationships with colleagues. Panamanians like to work with people they know, and pass on recommendations once they have established good business relations with a particular company. Being accepted within

Panama's business network will stand your company in excellent stead for its future dealings in Panama, and for this reason alone it is advisable to show your staying power, or potential commitment to the country.

In general, business proceedings in Panama follow a combination of three basic fundamentals: good manners, efficiency, and a relaxed, nonaggressive approach. There is usually a hierarchical structure to Panamanian business, and it is generally the top-level management that does the negotiating and makes the decisions. It is additionally worth remembering that business in the provincial areas does not reflect that of the city, and one should be prepared to be patient.

WORKING HOURS

Working hours vary a great deal throughout the business sector. Bank staff usually work from 8:00 a.m. until 3:00 p.m., but some banks close earlier, and others later. In addition, some are open on Saturday mornings, while others are not. For large transactions, corporate deals, and offshore accounts, appointments can be made in advance, and timing can be more flexible. However, city banks, no matter how large or well-staffed, often attract long lines of waiting customers.

Government businesses and offices usually open at 7:30 a.m. and close around 2:30 p.m., with a one-hour break for lunch. When visiting government organizations it is vital to arrive as early as possible, as state procedures can entail extensive administration. Workers may not be willing to start proceedings if you arrive late in the day and they anticipate there will not be enough time to complete, or even start, the task.

Private offices and businesses run the usual 9:00 a.m. (sometimes 10:00 a.m.) until 5:00 p.m. schedule, with a one-hour break for lunch. Although secretaries may leave the office, it is usual in corporate Panama for business hours and meetings to run beyond general office hours; however you should not rely on it. Appointments are the key to progressing your projects swiftly.

It is essential to enlist a local lawyer or advisor when doing business in Panama, and this will be expected. You should check as many credentials as possible when appointing a lawyer, and preferably use someone who has been recommended.

STATUS AND HIERARCHY

It is particularly important to be aware of hierarchy in Panama, as employees at the lower levels in business are not authorized to make decisions. Commerce is highly structured, and you need to know whom you are dealing with and how the company is run. A family-owned business, for example, may have employees who are competent and knowledgeable but who are not authorized to make major decisions for the company. In addition, government agencies usually have a group of decision makers who need to liaise together on the matter at hand. Decision making is nearly always done by top-level management, and when dealing with these executives it is imperative that foreigners use their own top-level management.

WHAT TO WEAR

A smart appearance is particularly important in Panama, where people are usually impeccably turned out. Business suits for both men and women are slightly more conservative than in Britain and the U.S.A. Men wear a tie and jacket, and women dress very conventionally in neat suits in unadventurous colors. Panamanians cannot accept those who do not dress well, and in business situations an untidy or revealing dress will reflect very badly on your company. Even simply entering a bank in Panama you are expected to be dressed reasonably, and open shirts and skimpy tops are frowned upon.

Unfortunately Panama's humid climate can sometimes make smart dressing very uncomfortable and this should be borne in mind when choosing an appropriate outfit. Although offices are usually air-conditioned, you may not be able to remove your jacket, at least during a formal first appointment.

A traditional garment in Panama is the *guayabera*. It is a long- or short-sleeved cotton tunic with vertically stitched embroidery. This remains acceptable formal business attire, and many older businessmen wear it because it is lightweight and cool. However, whereas older men look distinguished in the *guayabera*, it is regarded as out-of-date and is not generally worn by younger people. Nevertheless it generates true envy in those burdened with thick suits on humid city afternoons.

ADDRESSING AND GREETING PEOPLE

As we have noted, learning to speak some Spanish will improve your experience of the country. It is especially useful to master the basics of the language if you intend to do business in the country. This is not because you will be expected to conduct meetings and negotiations in Spanish—you will be expected to use a translator if necessary—but because it demonstrates respect for the country you are doing business in and for the people you are working with. If you can manage a little Spanish small talk, perhaps about the weather, or how you are pleased to be involved in business with this particular company, you will make a good impression. There are numerous books to help you with this.

On arrival it is polite to greet your colleagues with, "*Buenas días, Señor* (or *Señora*, or *Señorita*— Mr., Mrs., and Miss, respectively). First names are rarely used in top-level management discussions, unless you are very familiar with your host. Even with lower-level colleagues, you should always use formal address.

In Panama as in many Latin American countries, it is usual to have two surnames, the first being the father's surname, and the second the mother's maiden name. The second is not usually used in speech, although it may be printed on business cards and door and desk plaques. Señor Arauz Roca becomes simply Señor Arauz. However, using both is acceptable, and you may be told which is preferred.

Panamanian businessmen shake hands firmly but briefly on greeting each other. In situations where they know each other well, or where big deals are at hand, they may grasp the other's arm or hand with

the left hand during the handshake. Eye contact is kept throughout this brief but important introductory procedure. Women at higher-level management will usually also shake hands, rather than going for the usual kiss on one cheek, although this is not always so for lower-level management and close colleagues.

MAKING APPOINTMENTS

Always call in advance to make appointments, speaking to the secretary or to your main contact, as appropriate. E-mail has become a popular way of communicating, but this is only used for convenience once a good relationship has been established. On the whole, Panamanians prefer direct contact, and calling is better.

Panamanians can be very flexible, and canceling an appointment is acceptable as long as a new arrangement is made right away, or before the previously scheduled date has passed.

MEETINGS

Meetings are usually held in the office of your contact. Depending on the situation and business at hand, however, more elaborate arrangements may be made. Many hotels in Panama have business-meeting rooms supplied with essentials from presentation facilities to Internet hookups. Some hotels are able to arrange translators.

Always arrive punctually for business meetings, in spite of what anyone tells you about Panamanian timekeeping. Meetings start with an offer of refreshments and polite formalities, such as inquiries concerning your journey and health.

After this the course of Panamanian business meetings runs very much as meetings would in North America. However, Panamanians are more

relaxed than their northern counterparts, and interchanges before and after discussions and

negotiation are usually pleasant and friendly. As we have seen, it is good to aim at making a firm underlying relationship with your business partner that can extend to future opportunities for both companies. During meetings you should not try to speak Spanish if you have only a limited knowledge of the language, as you will only waste your hosts' precious time as you struggle and they attempt to understand you. It is far better to confirm in advance whether or not the people you are doing business with speak English, and, if not, to arrange for a translator to be present.

Panamanian businesspeople can be very proud of their achievements, and respond to flattery. Eye contact is very important in this case, as it demonstrates trust, as does relaxed body language, which will make clear to your partners that you are happy to be involved with them in their business.

PRESENTATIONS

Presentations follow a similar format to those in the U.S.A. Credibility is earned through confidence, and your presentation should be well rehearsed and thoroughly researched. A good business presentation will include one or two specialist colleagues to answer questions on the spot in depth. This also demonstrates the experience and knowledge of your company, which Panamanians will find reassuring. Panamanians will appreciate your flexibility during a formal presentation in taking impromptu queries and being willing to set aside your plans to address their initial questions. They will not usually interrupt a presentation, but should this happen try to maintain complete ease with the situation; remember, good manners and a relaxed style are most important in Panama. Throughout the presentation maintain eye contact with all the

members of the audience, and aim specific points and conclusions to the top-level management present. All of these gestures on your part—providing specialist answers to questions, willingness to explore your hosts' concerns, and retaining a level of spontaneity—will show that you have the commitment and interest that Panamanians want from international business relationships.

NEGOTIATING AND CONTRACTS

Negotiations in Panama tend to be flexible and can be relatively informal. This does not mean that they are any easier to conduct than in other countries, but that Panamanians have a more relaxed business style. Foreigners should remember that Panamanians are less direct than Europeans, and enjoy subtle negotiations rather than hard-hitting, straight-to-the-point talks. Additionally, Panamanians do not appreciate the know-it-all attitude often adopted by North Americans. Good business practice in Panama requires a level playing field between the parties and should be neither confrontational nor condescending. Patronizing behavior can be offensive and will ultimately, and understandably, result in a poor outcome. Because trading is traditional in Panama, a merchant mind-set dominates negotiations and securing a deal seems to be an inbuilt national skill.

In the case of smaller businesses, or those outside the city, this may not apply. However, many Panamanians today are sure of their own strengths, particularly in regard to land, much of which has been acquired by foreign investors. Gone are the days when locals were impressed with the sight of wealth and deals would be swiftly made, sometimes to their detriment. Some property owners may feel the situation does not warrant extensive discussion; they are not frightened of losing a deal and can on occasion be unwilling to negotiate. They may be prepared to sit and wait for as long as it takes to get an answer, well aware that it is usually the foreign visitor who needs to hurry. This is evidence of a more confident Panamanian people.

With all negotiations it is vital to gain trust and respect within the business domain. It is important to communicate your staying power and commitment. In true "family" style, many Panamanians believe that good commercial relationships last, and can be beneficial to both parties in the future.

Panama's Civil Code (endorsed in 1914) follows that of Spain. Foreign law contracts, including Anglo-American, are also recognized and Panamanian corporate law is now heavily influenced by U.S. and British cases. However, it is vital that a reputable lawyer oversees your business contracts as these are only legally binding, respected, and enforceable in court if the contract contains no provisions contrary to Panamanian law. It is perhaps worth noting that the legal process can be lengthier than that in the U.S.A. or Britain, but it is certainly cheaper.

WOMEN IN BUSINESS

In 1999 Mireya Moscoso became Panama's first female president, which in itself speaks volumes for the advancement of women in Panama. It has highlighted the ability of Panamanian women to function as well as their male colleagues in business. However, the underlying Latin *machismo* remains as ingrained in commerce as in the home, and there are still relatively few women in top-level management and CEO positions in Panama.

This said, Panamanians have realized the benefits of employing women, and many business executives themselves will in fact admit that women work as well as, and in many respects better than, their male equivalents. Panamanian women at work are reported by some senior business executives to be less likely than men to display arrogance, and to work harder for longer. Hence, in Panama you will find plenty of women in middle-to-upper management, and some companies are actually more likely to employ a woman than a man at certain management levels. Women are especially well accepted in business circles in Panama City.

In Panama City, today's young women are realizing that they can further their careers by staying at university rather than becoming young housewives as their parents' and grandparents' generations did. Such ambition is encouraged in the middle and upper classes, although girls in lower- and working-class societies still tend to become mothers at a younger age and are more likely to become unskilled workers. Outside the cities, a woman's main role is still that of housewife, and while many do go out to work, many others are still expected to take sole care of the children.

Foreign businesswomen arriving in Panama are most unlikely to be confronted with hostility because of their sex. Male colleagues can occasionally appear rather condescending toward women in business, but in general modern businessmen in Panama will be more interested in getting down to the task at hand.

BUSINESS ENTERTAINING

In Panama it is unusual to discuss business over food, and meetings are usually restricted to offices and formal settings. If you have a straightforward deal you wish to get under way as rapidly as possible, it is best to meet in an office. However, lunch can be suggested, although discussions would be lighter and less formal, and this can be an excellent way to develop friendly relations with Panamanian people and companies. Time can be taken to discuss how business in Panama functions, and for both parties to elaborate on their own businesses and ideas.

Dinner with Panamanians is not as lengthy as in some Latin American countries, although it will almost certainly run to three courses and coffee. The party who initiated the occasion will be expected to pay. Gifts are not usually expected, although a small gift will be welcomed, especially something from the visitor's country, such as a typical whiskey or a bottle of wine. The dinner guest will be expected to return the honor, and should extend a reciprocal invitation after the meal.

Business breakfasts are generally reserved for politicians and other elite groups, and it is against Panamanian etiquette to invite a potential client or business partner to breakfast on a first meeting. Breakfasts and dinners can be suggested once you have developed some degree of intimacy or trust with your colleagues.

"GREASING THE WHEELS"

Bribery has been a part of business life in Panama, as in many Latin American countries, for years, and you should expect to come across it at some point. Not only that, but you may find yourself offered the opportunity of making bribes yourself. This is generally frowned on today, although some people make and accept bribes without question. The new Torrijos government has announced a policy of zero tolerance on business bribery, threatening jail for those caught in the act. While this is not expected to change things immediately and underhand measures may continue to go unnoticed, it is a start, and a few minor charges have been brought.

There are three possible outcomes from taking or offering a bribe: you will get caught and go to jail; you will pay and get no benefit; or you will pay and get what you expected. But, should the third possibility occur, you may find that you are on a slippery slope and that hidden costs eat up your profits. Bribery is illegal, and should be avoided or refused.

chapter nine

COMMUNICATING

LANGUAGE

The official language of Panama is Spanish. Latin American Spanish varies slightly in dialect from country to country, and while locals can usually spot the differences, some foreign Spanish speakers cannot. It takes time and practice to pick up on phrases that are particularly Panamanian.

Panamanian Spanish is very clear, and Panamanians are well spoken in formal situations. Informally, especially among young people, the language can be more confusing, added to which every Latin American country has some of its own slang. Panamanians have a trick of cutting a word in two and switching the halves back to front. For example, "*mopri*" (used informally for "mate," or "good friend") is taken from "*primo*" (cousin); and "*Q'sopa*?," used throughout Panama's younger generations, comes from "*Que pasa*?" meaning "What's happening?" and is used as an informal greeting. Other words may just be shortened and joined together, for example "*polante*" ("I am going"), taken from "*para adelante*" (going forward).

Speaking Spanish

Spanish is a very attractive language, and is relatively easy to learn once you've mastered the pronunciation. Perhaps the most confusing part for many English speakers is to come to grips with learning genders, but these also seem to fall into place with practice. Although many Panamanians in the city and in Caribbean areas speak English, locals appreciate visitors who speak Spanish, even if it's just a few words in everyday situations. It is best to dive in and have a go, as it is a great way to break the ice between strangers. The more you converse with the locals, the more you will pick up as you go.

Other Languages

Panama's Indians have different languages, and many other languages that once existed in Panama have unfortunately died out over the centuries. Books are available on the Kuna language, and visitors planning to spend time in the San Blas area should consider finding out more. Other Indian languages are less well documented, and most Indians who intermingle with mainstream society also speak Spanish.

The Afro–Antillean descendants on Panama's northern shores speak what is known in the country as *Guari Guari* (pronounced Wari Wari), a Creole dialect using Spanish, English, and Indian vernacular. At first it seems as though *Guari Guari* is predominantly English, but this is deceptive, as the patois mix is difficult, and at the end of the conversation you may be left guessing at the translation.

Probably the most locally famous expression is "*Whappen?*" ("What's happening?"). This phrase has been adopted by residents, regardless of their ancestry, from Colón and Bocas del Toro right up to the Limón region of Costa Rica's Caribbean.

BODY LANGUAGE

Panamanians are in the main relaxed, optimistic, convivial, and happy to welcome visitors to their country. However, they are also very formal, and regard good manners as essential. Body language should reflect this mixture of warmth and respect. Paying due attention in conversation is important, and glancing absently around, changing the subject, or moving away would be rude and offensive.

On both meeting and parting, it is appropriate for two men to shake hands, and for two women, or a woman and a man, to kiss once on the cheek.

After the initial welcome, people revert to their own private space and no more physical contact is necessary; in fact it can be misunderstood.

HUMOR

Slapstick humor is popular in Panama; ironic or black humor is not so common and can on occasion be misunderstood. Panamanians can be excellent storytellers and in social situations jokes can be lengthy narratives that are accentuated with body movement made funnier by the teller's building fervor. Generally, jokes are very popular, and can be made about any aspect of life except, of course, the family and religion, which would be insulting.

THE MEDIA
TV and Radio

There are several local TV channels. The most popular are Telemetro, TVN Canal 2, RPC Televisión, and FETV Canal 5. Direct TV (satellite) is now very popular among those who can afford it.

The main radio stations include RPC, Radio Nacional de Panamá (La Voz del Estado), Stereo 89, Rock n Pop (106.7 FM), Super Estación Panamá (92.1 FM), and Fabulosa Estereo (100.5 FM).

The Press

Print media in Panama suffered from censorship throughout the Noriega years. In fact in 1989 Noriega shut down *La Prensa* (the main newspaper whose stance was critical of the government), along with a number of radio stations. After Noriega's demise *La Prensa* and several other newspapers reopened.

Today there are six main news titles in Panama. The top qualities are mostly independent, and include *El Panamá América, El Siglo*, and the popular *La Prensa. Diario el Universal de Panamá* and *La Estrella de Panamá* tend to be right-wing, although they have both been seen to change sides politically over the years. Panama's independent tabloid *La Critica* is the most widely read by Panamanians and is often the first to print images from the country's most disturbing news on its front page.

English-Language Publications

In Panama City many English-language magazines can be found in larger pharmacies and some department stores. In other areas the choice is limited to a locally published edition of the *Miami Herald*, which is distributed throughout most populated areas of the country. The *Panama News* is an online English-language newspaper that concentrates on news, politics, and events in Panama. There are some locally printed regional news sheets, mostly written by expatriates.

SERVICES
Mail

The postal service in Panama is generally good, although there are no door-to-door deliveries and you will need to use a central mailbox address, or have your mail, with the direction "Entrega General" and your name, sent to the post office in your area. Neither are there any mailboxes for sending mail, and all postcards, letters, and parcels should be taken directly to the post office.

In Panama City, post offices can be hard to find. There is a main post office in Plaza Concordia on Via España, and another in El Dorado shopping mall. Hours are 7:00 a.m. to 5:45 p.m., Monday to Friday, with most city post offices closing at 5:00 p.m. on Saturdays. Provincial towns have a central post office, which usually closes earlier in the afternoon and may or may not have a Saturday service. Regular mail to Europe can take up to ten days; to North America it is slightly less. For parcels, or more important items, you may want to use a shipping or express parcel service for speed and peace of mind. DHL and Federal Express have offices in Panama.

Telephone

Panama's country code is 507. There are no area codes and to dial from within the country you simply enter the seven-digit number. Cell phones usually have 6 as a prefix.

The telephone service has been much improved over the last decade. In tourist locations and some hotels, international phones requiring a credit card are available. These can be very expensive, and it is always cheaper to call from a pay phone than from a hotel.

Pay phones are blue or yellow, and can be used with cards and sometimes coins. It is best to carry  a phone card as most use cards and not coins. Phone cards can be bought at supermarkets and small food stores. There are different cards for local calls, international calls, and cell phones. Cards for local and international calls either have a PIN, which you need to enter on dialing the central number, or are simply inserted into the card slot. Coin phones accept twenty-five-cent, ten-cent, and five-cent coins.

Call centers now offer excellent international rates that are far cheaper than international calling cards, but are still found mainly in the cities, in Internet locations; most are around Via España and Via Veneto.

Owing to the volume of business conducted in Panama, it is possible to rent cell phones, but this can be expensive. You may find it is better to buy a Panamanian SIM card for your mobile phone, which usually comes with set minutes; credit can then be replenished with prepay cards, available in supermarkets. The main companies in Panama are Cable and Wireless and Bell South. You will need a tri-band (850/1800/1900) telephone, which has not been locked to a specific network.

USEFUL TELEPHONE NUMBERS

Directory Inquiries 102 (operators speak Spanish only)

International Call Via Operator 106

Police (*Policía*) 104

Fire Brigade (*Bomberos*) 103

Ambulances (*Ambulancias*) 103

Ambulances for:

Seguro Social 229-1133

Santo Tomas 227-4122

Cruz Roja 228-2187

Cruz Blanca 270-0231

Alerta (private emergency service):

Panama 263-4522

Colón 441-1151

Computers and the Internet

Laptop users are usually able to plug in at Internet cafés and some of the better hotels. Panama uses

110 volts, so you may need an AC adaptor and a plug adaptor. Additionally, you should bear in mind the electric current can occasionally be erratic, and a "surge protector" is recommended.

Internet connections are excellent in Panama's main cities and in some tourist spots. Internet Service Providers use A-DSL or TV cable-modem technology. High-speed Internet areas are growing  although customary dial-up services are still used throughout the country.

Tourism is certainly responsible for a sharp rise in Internet facilities in Panama, but many government establishments offer reduced rates to locals. Children and young people are encouraged to use computers both in and outside school. In Panama City and many towns, from the lower-middle class up most young people have had some computer instruction. The emergence of the Internet has fed the need for computer literacy, and it is common to see young people around the country teaching themselves computer basics so that they can use the Internet to contact friends.

CONCLUSION

Panama is an exceptionally beautiful part of the tropics, and there are some spectacular areas left to explore. This, combined with the Panamanian commitment to modernization, makes it not only a place full of exciting possibilities, but also a newly vulnerable country. The rate of construction continues apace, as does the alarming rate of logging in the Darién, and mining throughout the country. Panama still has precious and unique resources that, without some forward thinking, may be lost to future generations.

Visitors will be delighted with their reception in Panama. Despite the political turmoil of recent years and the ill repute this has occasionally caused, the Panamanians display no bitterness, and wholeheartedly welcome foreigners to the country. What will immediately strike you is their warmth, sociability, and genuine interest in you. You will discover not just the beauty of the countryside, but the variety of regional and local ways of life. The mix of rich and poor is always apparent and thought-provoking—a classic Panamanian scene is a group of native people fishing at dawn in small dugouts with rice-sack sails, near large, expensive catamarans and speedboats fueling up to take tourists on a trip.

In this guide we have set out to introduce you to the surprising breadth and depth of Panamanian culture. You will soon discover for yourself the full pleasure of encountering the Panamanian people.

Useful Web Sites

Government Bodies and Tourist Information

Instituto Panameño de Panamá (IPAT) Panama´s Tourist Board.
Located at Centro de Convenciones ATLAPA, Via Israel, San Francisco,
Panama City. Tel. (507) 226 7000 www.ipat.gob.pa (Spanish)

www.visitpanama.com (English/Spanish)

www.municipio.gob.pa (Spanish)

www.panamainfo.com (English/Spanish)

www.panama-guide.com (English)

Environmental Sites

www.ancon.org/Anconweb/intro.html (Spanish)

www.stri.com (English/Spanish)

Colón Free Zone

www.zonalibredecolon.com.pa (English/Spanish)

Museums

www.panamacanalmuseum.org (English)

www.panamaviejo.org (Spanish)

www.biomuseopanama.org (English/Spanish)

www.macpanama.org (Spanish)

Regional Sites

www.bocasdeltoro.com (English)

www.chiriqui.org (English/Spanish)

www.chitrenet.net (Spanish)

www.lossantosonline.net (Spanish)

Further Reading

Barry, Tom, and John Lindsay-Poland with Marco Gandásegui and Peter Simonson. *Inside Panama*. Albuquerque, N.M.: Interhemispheric Resource Center, 1995.

Howard, Christopher. *Living and Investing in Panama*. San José, Costa Rica: Costa Rica Books, 2004.

Labrut, Michèle. *Getting to Know Panama*. El Dorado, Panama: Focus Publications, 1997.

Le Carré, John. *The Tailor of Panama*. New York: Ballantine Books, 1997.

Lindsay-Poland, John. *Emperors in the Jungle: The Hidden History of the U.S. in Panama*. Durham, N.C.: Duke University Press, 2003.

McCullough, David. *The Path Between the Seas*. New York: Simon & Schuster, 1977.

Prebble, John. *The Darien Disaster*. London: Secker & Warburg, 1968; London: Pimlico, 2002.

Ridgely, Robert S., and John A Gwynne. *A Guide to the Birds of Panama*. Princeton, N.J.: Princeton University Press, 1992.

St. Louis, Regis. *Lonely Planet Panama*. Melbourne: 2004.

Woods, Sarah. *Panama: The Bradt Travel Guide*. Chalfont St Giles, Bucks, U.K.: Bradt, 2005.

Spanish. A Complete Course. New York: Living Language, 2005.

In-Flight Spanish. New York: Living Language, 2001.

Fodor's Spanish for Travelers (CD Package). New York: Living Language, 2005.

Index

culture smart! **panama**

Acknowledgments

I would like to thank K. C. Hardin and Ramón Ricardo Arias for their helpful comments. Extra special thanks go to Anthony Gordon, Esme McGinnes, Claire Barnham for her editing assistance, Ricardo Hernandez, and, in particular, to Brixie Indigo for her inspiring wisdom.